Progress English

Level 3-4

LIZ CLARK

Heinemann Educational Publishers
Halley Court, Jordan Hill, Oxford, OX2 8EJ
A part of Harcourt Education Limited

Heinemann is a registered trademark of Harcourt Education Limited

First published 2003
07 06 05 04 03
10 9 8 7 6 5 4 3 2 1

ISBN 0 435 22122 1

Designed by hicksdesign
Produced by Bridge Creative Services Limited
Printed and bound in Italy by Printer Trento Srl.

Copyright permissions sought by Jackie Newman

Original illustrations © Heinemann Educational Publishers 2002

Illustrations: Julian Mosedale: pages 7, 11, 19, 111, 125, Kathy Baxendale: pages 8, 52, 95, 99, 106, 122–123, 124–125,126–127, Abigail Conway: pages 12, 21, 58, 62, 64, 89, Nick Schon: pages 14, 22–23, 45, 46, 48, 107, Martin Ursell: pages 10, 33, 35, 41, 43, 75, 76, 80, Chris Brown: pages 28, 30, 31, Andrew Morris: pages 36–37, 39, 102, Alice Englander: page 103

The publishers would like to thank the following for permission to reproduce photographs on the pages noted.

P17 Mersey TV Publicity; p49 Rex Features/Cumulus, Kobal/Columbia; p56 Bridgeman Art Library/Prado, Madrid; p86 Photodisc; p93 Ronal Grant Archive/Disney/Pixar; p90 Eidos

Tel: 01865 888058 www.heinemann.co.uk

Welcome to Progress English!

What's the book about?

This book has been designed to help you become a more effective reader and writer and to help you enjoy your English lessons more.

How will it do this?

As you work through the units, you will pick up 'tricks of the trade' that will help you improve on all the skills a good reader and writer uses. Before you know it, you may even be writing a new best-seller to rival the Harry Potter books!

What if I'm already working on these skills?

You may already be focusing on some of these skills in Progress Unit lessons. This book will help you build on these skills as well as encouraging you to take them further and produce a range of interesting pieces of work that will leave your readers hungry for more!

Do I have to work through all the units?

No. Each unit is designed to be used on its own and targets different reading and writing skills. However, the more units you study the better your reading and writing skills will become.

What are all those symbols (icons) in the margins for?

These are to help you (and your teacher) work through the unit and know what kind of activity you are about to do or to highlight important learning points.

Just to help you the icons are shown below with an explanation of what they mean:

 this shows the main skills you are exploring in a section

 this is there to remind you of points you already know but might have forgotten

 this indicates a quick challenge at the beginning of a lesson to get your brain racing

 this indicates the main part of the lesson where you will be expected to work individually, with a partner or in a small group

 this shows you where you will need to work with a partner or a small group as you will need to discuss ideas to be able to complete the task

 this summarises the main skills you have explored in a section and helps you remember the most important points

 this shows you that there are worksheets in the Teacher's Resource Pack to support this activity – your teacher may give you the worksheet to help you complete a task

 this shows you where there is an activity to develop your reading skills

 this shows you where there is an activity to develop your writing skills

I hope that you enjoy the variety of tasks and challenges in **Progress English** as it helps you to develop effective reading and writing skills that will wow your English teacher.

Liz Clark

Contents

Section A Sharpen those skills!

UNIT 1 Piecing together the puzzle

How good a reading detective are you? Test your skills of inference and deduction by investigating the fiction texts in this unit. Can you find the hidden meanings, clue in to the characters and solve the mysteries? Turn to page 7 to take up the challenge.

UNIT 2 Let me entertain you!

This unit introduces you to the secret 'tricks of the trade' in writing exciting and imaginative narratives and invites you to add your own creations to the writers' 'Hall of Fame'.

UNIT 3 Read all about it – the facts and the fiction

There are lots of non-fiction texts waiting to be read in this unit. When you've read them, can you sort out the facts from the fiction, the main points from the unimportant? A chance to show off your reading and note-making skills.

UNIT 4 All aboard for a magical mystery tour

A whistle-stop tour of detailed descriptions, impressive information texts and excellent explanations. Then it's over to you to create your very own terrific tour guide.

Acknowledgements

The publishers gratefully acknowledge the following for permission to reproduce copyright material. Whilst every effort has been made to trace the copyright holders, in cases where this has proved unsuccessful or if any have inadvertently been overlooked, the publishers will be pleased to make the necessary arrangement at the first opportunity.

BBC1 and Channel 4 TV listings from Oxford Times 16th August, Reprinted with the kind permission of BBC and Channel 4. Extract from *Knights of the Kitchen Table* by Jon Scieszka, copyright © 1991 by Jon Scieszka. Used by permission of Viking Penguin, an imprint of Penguin Putnam Books for Young Readers, a division of Penguin Putnam Inc. All rights reserved. Extract from *I'm Telling You, They're Aliens* by Jeremy Strong, published by Puffin. Reprinted with permission of David Higham Associates Limited. Extracts from *Machine Gunners* by Robert Westall, published by Macmillan. Reprinted with permission of Macmillan. *The Case of the Ruined Roses* by Esther B. Wheeler and an extract from *The Darkmaster's Challenge* by Michael Mallory appeared on MysteryNet.com Kids Mysteries Site. Copyright © 1996, 2002 Newfront Productions Inc. Used with permission. Extract from *Harry Potter & The Philosopher's Stone* by J. K. Rowling published by Bloomsbury. Copyright © J. K. Rowling 1997. and extract from *Harry Potter & the Goblet of Fire* by J. K. Rowling, published by Bloomsbury. Copyright © 2000 J. K. Rowling, and an extract from *Harry Potter & The Chamber of Secrets* by J. K. Rowling, Copyright © J.K. Rowling, Reprinted with permission of Christopher Little Literary Agency, London. Extract from *The Lion, The Witch and the Wardrobe* by C. S. Lewis. Copyright © C. S. Lewis Pte Ltd, 1950. Extract reprinted with permission of C. S. Lewis Company Limited. Extract from 'Woman and Home' by Robert Westall, from *The Call and Other Stories* published by Puffin. Copyright © Robert Westall 1989. Reprinted with permission of Laura Cecil Literary Agency, London. Extract from *Dr. Franklin's Island* by Ann Halam, published by Orion Children's Books. Reprinted with permission of The Orion Publishing Group Limited. Extracts from *The Weirdstone of Brisingamen* by Alan Garner, published by HarperCollins Publishers. Reprinted with permission of HarperCollins Publishers. Extract from *Holes* by Louis Sachar, published by Bloomsbury. Reprinted with permission of Bloomsbury. Extract from *The Magical Worlds of Harry Potter* by David Colbert (Puffin 2001) Copyright © David Colbert 2001. Reprinted with permission of Penguin Group UK. Extract from *www.thenewspaper.org.uk* reprinted with the kind permission of Young Media Limited. 'Grasshopper Gumbo' from *www.lavamind.com*. Extracts from *The Greek Gazette/Medieval Messenger* reproduced by permission of Usborne Publishing, 83–85 Saffron Hill, London EC1N 8RT UK. Copyright © Usborne Publishing Limited 1997/1996. Extract from *Horrible Histories: The Blitzed Brits* written by Terry Deary, illustrated by Martin Brown. Text Copyright © Terry Deary, Illustrations Copyright © Martin Brown. First published by Scholastic Children's Books and reproduced by permission of Scholastic Ltd. Extract from *Count Drawcula's Cartoon Fun* by Frank Rogers, published by Scholastic. Reprinted by permission of Caroline Sheldon Literary Agency on behalf of the author. Characters – Gromit, and Characters – Wallace, found on Wallace & Gromit Online. Copyright © 2002 Aardman/Wallace & Gromit Ltd. Reproduced with the kind permission of Aardman. Extracts *Cadbury Chocolate Factory* and *Cadbury World* Opening in July 2002' from the Cadbury Confectionary Ltd website www.cadbury.co.nz. Reprinted with the kind permission of Cadburys New Zealand. Extract from *Charlie and the Chocolate Factory* by Roald Dahl, published by Penguin. Reprinted with permission of David Higham Associates Limited. *Campaign Tips* from www.rspca.org.uk. Reprinted with the kind permission of the RSPCA. Extracts from www.chessington.co.uk. Reprinted with the kind permission of Chessington World of Adventures. Extracts from *Camelot Theme Park Leaflet.* This leaflet is the 2002 edition and is therefore out of date. Some changes may happen for 2003 ie prices and times etc. Reprinted with the kind permisson of Camelot Theme Park. Image of Lara Croft © Core Design. Reprinted with the kind permission of Core Design. *John Donaldson Age 23* Advert for Barnardos. Reprinted with the kind permission of Barnardos. *Oxy in the Shower* advert, reprinted with the kind permission of the Ogilvy Group. Extract from *Test of the Twins* by Margaret Weis and Tracy Hickman (Penguin Books, 1987) Copyright © Margaret Weis and Tracy Hickman 1987. Reprinted with permission of Penguin Group UK. Extract from 'Feeding the Dog' by Susan Price, from *Here Lies Price* published by Faber and Faber Limited. Reprinted with permission of Faber and Faber Limited. Extract from *Crossing* by Dennis Hamley. Copyright © Dennis Hamley. Reprinted with the kind permission of the author. Extract from *Nightmare in Blue* by Fredric Brown. Copyright © 1954, by Fredric Brown, copyright 1982 by the Estate of Fredric Brown. Reprinted by permission of the Estate and its agent. Extract from 'Spider's Web' from *Tales from Africa* by Kathleen Arnott, published by Oxford University Press in 1962. Reprinted with permission of Oxford University Press. 'The Christmas Gift' by Hugh Oliver, found in *The Oxford Book of Christmas Stories* edited by Dennis Pepper, and published by Oxford University Press.

Piecing together the puzzle

In this unit you will use your 'detective' skills to work out what you think is going to happen in a range of stories. You will investigate the clues a writer leaves to help you, the reader, puzzle out the endings.

You'll also think about how a writer creates characters and settings so we can paint a picture of them in our minds and think of them as real people and places.

So ... get reading and puzzle it out!

1.1 A picture develops

Key puzzle

- What skills do we need to build up pictures to help us to understand the stories we read?

Remember!

- **Images** are the pictures we paint in our minds using clues (evidence) from pictures and words in stories.

Super sleuths

1. Look at the items below. They were found in a briefcase that was handed in to a local police station. What do these items suggest to you about the kind of person they belong to?

1.1

2. Now copy and complete the grid on the next page, explaining what the items tell you about the person who has lost the case. Some of this has already been done for you.

Evidence	What this tells us about the owner of the case
Diary with red circle around date Friday 13th November	He has something important thing to do on Friday. Could be a birday or a deadline.
Expensive pen and pencil set	Owner might have a lot of money to spend on luxury things. They keep things tidy.
Torn cinema ticket	Maybe for an alibi
Car keys with a key fob with letter H on it	Possibly his name begins H.
A brown envelope containing £5000 in used notes	He possibly stole them. He might have been paid for a job or drugs, ransom money.
A business card for a private detective	He might have rented a private detective, or he might be one himself.
A local newspaper with words and pictures cut out	To write a ransom note

3. Now, with a partner, suggest reasons why you think the briefcase was abandoned.
4. Feedback your ideas to the rest of the class.

Collecting the evidence

5. Read the extract below. As you read, think carefully about how we build up a picture of *The Book*.

> I pulled back the black and gold paper and lifted it up.
>
> 'It's a … It's a …'
>
> 'Aw, it's just a book,' said Fred, rolling my baseball around the table.
>
> And it was a book. But it wasn't like any book I had ever seen before. It was such a dark, dark blue that it looked almost black, like the sky at night. It had gold stars and moons along the back edge, and twisting silver designs on the front and back that looked like writing from a long time ago.
>
> I looked closer and read the title. *'The Book.'*
>
> 'Great name for a book,' said Sam.
>
> Mum looked relieved.
>
> 'Hey, let me see.' Fred dropped the baseball on the kitchen table and grabbed *The Book* out of my hand.
>
> 'Wait a minute, Fred. Be careful.'
>
> Fred opened *The Book.*
>
> There was a picture of a guy on a black horse standing on a path at the edge of a small clearing. He was dressed from head to toe in black armour like you see in those books about knights and castles. He didn't look very happy.
>
> From *The Knights of the Kitchen Table* by Jon Scieszka, from *The Time Warp Trio*

6. Look at the different pictures of how *The Book* might look. Which one is closest to how you imagine it to look? Why?

7. Now draw up a grid like the one opposite, showing how you made your decision.

What I know about The Book	*Line number*	*The words (quotation) that tell me this*	*Which picture does this information rule out?*

Solution to key puzzle

- What skills do we need to build up pictures to help us to understand the stories we read?

8. With a partner, brainstorm all the skills you have used to build up pictures for these tasks.

9. Share your ideas with the rest of the class and make a note of the three most important skills.

Congratulations! You have successfully completed part one of the 'reading detective' trail!

1.2 Making an impression

Key puzzles

- What 'tricks of the trade' do writers use to help us understand what kind of person a character is?
- How do we know what a character is feeling at any point in the story?

Remember!

- **Characteristics** are the different elements of a character's personality.
- When we **predict** we are making guesses based on clues/ evidence in the text.

Challenge your partner

Little Red Riding Hood　Robin Hood　Cinderella　Quasimodo　Humpty Dumpty

1. With a partner, look at the first classic character. Take it in turns to think of a word that describes that character. The first person to hesitate or stop loses and the other person scores one point. Keep going until you have described all the characters.
2. Look at the different pictures again and think of clues that would help other pairs to guess which one you were looking at. (Try to start with more difficult clues.)

   For example, if you were looking at a picture of Batman:

   - This character fights evil.
   - This character sometimes works with a partner.
   - This character is helpful.
   - This character has super powers.

3. Once you have worked out some clues for a couple of the characters, challenge another pair to work out your clues. If they guess and get it wrong, they automatically lose!

Creating characters

We often work out what a character is like by the way the writer describes them.

4. Read the extract below and over the page. Think about what we learn about the narrator, Rob, and his neighbours.

I knew they were aliens the first moment I saw them. I could feel it in my body. I got this kind of creeping sensation, as if ants were slowly crawling up and down the inside of my bones. You know how when you see an old bone, it's all sort of hollow down the middle, like a tunnel? Well, that's where these ants were crawling, up and down, and it worried me.

Nobody had seen a removal van. Nobody had seen the new neighbours move in. One moment they weren't there, and the next moment they were. It was just like *Star Trek*, you know, when they get beamed from one place to another. Only nobody saw it happen.

I was in my bedroom doing my violin practice when I noticed him. He looked like a typical human, but, I mean, what a give-away! Aliens coming to our planet *always* look like ordinary humans, otherwise you'd spot them a mile off and go around screaming 'Help! Aliens! Aliens invading Planet Earth!' (Well, I would anyhow.)

He looked about fourteen. He was lanky and there was something threatening about the way he just stood there. He was wearing shorts, the really baggy kind that come down past your knees. He had funny hair too. Well, it wasn't exactly funny. *Weird* would be a better word. It was very short, and it had a zigzag pattern shaved into it, as if the hairdresser had had some terrifying scare and his electric razor had slipped.

I guess it was because his hair was so short that his ears stuck out. They were extraordinary. They sat on the sides of his head like twin satellite dishes. I mean, with ears like those he could pick up messages from deep space, let alone satellite TV.

Anyhow, by this time, I had goose pimples all over, which is a sure sign that I was seriously scared. I was staring down at this boy and then his mother came out and called to him. She was pretty and well-dressed, but she looked even more worried than me, as if she had some dreadful secret – which she did, of course. There was something else too.

She had The Mark *upon her.*

There was a dark blotch just below her throat. I could tell it wasn't a bruise or anything like that. I zipped downstairs, borrowed Dad's bird-watching binoculars and zoomed in. You know what that mark was? It was a star cluster, a constellation! She might just as well have carried a sticker on her head, with the name of her planet written on it.

From *I'm Telling You, They're Aliens!* by Jeremy Strong

5. Imagine you are going to meet Rob (the narrator) for the first time. What kind of person would you be expecting to meet? Brainstorm your ideas, showing your thoughts on Rob and your reasons. Use the example below to start you off.

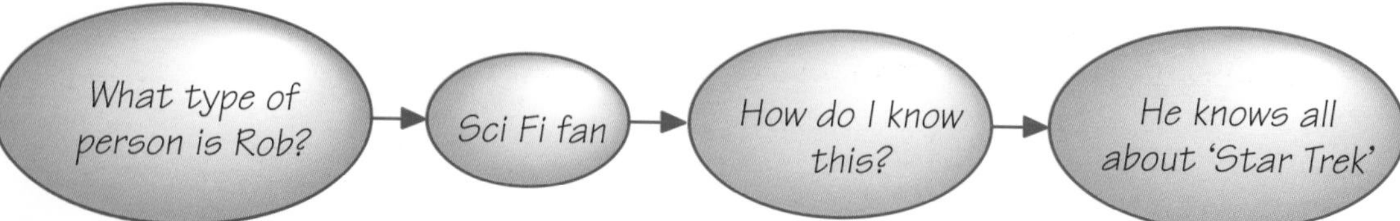
What type of person is Rob?
Sci Fi fan
How do I know this?
He knows all about 'Star Trek'

It is also important to try to understand how a character is feeling at any point in a story. This helps them to seem more real to us.

In the extract below, from the *Machine Gunners*, set during the Second World War, Chas McGill is trying to cover up the fact he has stolen a German machine gun. His bitter enemy is Boddser Brown.

6. Read the extract. Which words and phrases help us to understand how Chas is feeling at this point?

'Right, boys. Open your English exercise books. I want an essay on *War Souvenirs.*'

Silence fell, but for the scratch of pens. Chas knew how he could gain one hour, and no more. And that hour would be his last chance to save the gun. He stuck his tongue out of the corner of his mouth and wrote.

I used to have the best collection of war souvenirs in this town. I have eleven incendiary-bomb fins, twenty-six spent bullets, eighteen pieces of shrapnel, including one piece a foot long, and fifty empty cartridge-cases including ten in clips that my Dad's friend who is in the Armed Trawlers gave me.

But now my collection is second-best, because Boddser Brown in 3B has beaten me. He has a 3.7 inch nose-cone, and a pongy German flier's helmet, and lots of German money with Hitler's face on it, and a picture of a German girl in pigtails, called Mein Liebling. I wish I knew how he got these things, becos he's beating me hollow, and if I can't beat him soon, I shall have to give up and start collecting cigarette cards instead.

The bell went for the end of the lesson.

'Close your books and pass them up,' said Mr Liddell.

There was a storm of protest.

'But sir, we haven't finished. Can't we finish it for homework?'

'No, pass them up.' You could tell Mr Liddell couldn't wait to get his hand on those books. Chas grinned to himself. He owed Boddser Brown that one.

From *The Machine Gunners* by Robert Westall

7. What words do you think sum up Chas's feelings best?

Solution to key puzzles

- What 'tricks of the trade' do writers use to help us understand what kind of person a character is?
- How do we know what a character is feeling at any point in the story?

8. Imagine you are writing a brief 'key points list' for a new author on how to create interesting characters that we understand and believe in. What would be your five 'key points'?

Make sure you include information on the characters' thoughts and feelings.

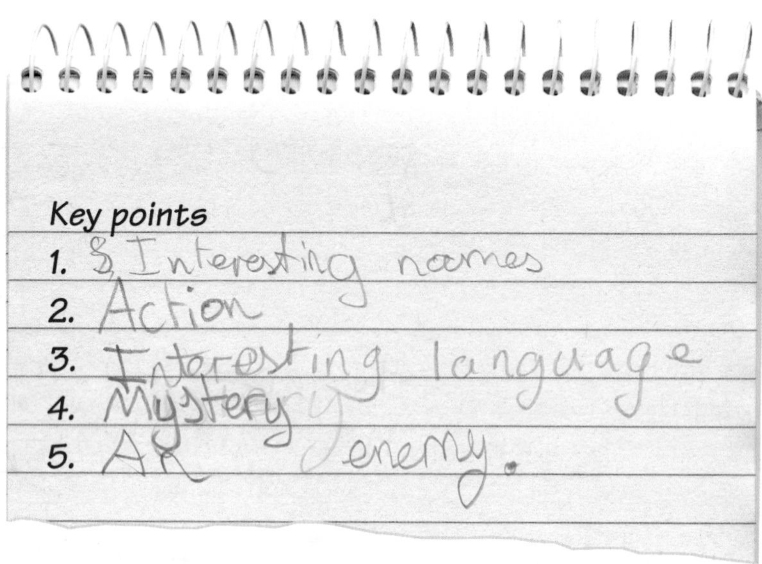

Key points
1. Interesting names
2. Action
3. Interesting language
4. Mystery
5. enemy.

Challenge part two complete! You have now successfully completed the 'Understanding characters' stage of the 'reading detective' trail!

1.3 Clues, clues, clues!

Key puzzle

- How do writers help their readers work out what has already happened in a story and predict what might be going to happen?

Remember!

- **Prediction** means making guesses based on what we know.
- **Retrospective** means looking back at what might have happened before.

Telling the future

1. Imagine you are going to predict what was going to happen in your favourite TV programme. Brainstorm all the words you can think of that you might use to start off each sentence, e.g. *Perhaps ...*

2. Put together a class list of these 'signpost' words.

Checking out the clues

3. Read the extract below. What clues are there to show what has happened before? What do you think will happen next?

Then lightning struck my room. That's the only way I can describe it. A sudden flash knocked me over and the next thing I knew, Randy and I were on our hands and knees in some kind of a hot, stuffy, stone room. There were lit torches and I could see picture writing on the walls. 'Egyptian hieroglyphics!' I said. 'This is totally nuts, but we're inside a pyramid!'

But he was too busy screaming to hear me. I turned and saw what he was screaming at. Leaning against one wall was a mummy case, and the lid was creaking open! When it opened all the way, the wrinkled bone-bag inside raised its head and looked at us!

We ran into each other at first but then toward a passageway that led out of the chamber. From behind us we heard footsteps ... the mummy was chasing us!

From *The Darkmaster's Challenge*, from MysteryNet's Kids Mysteries

R

1.3

4. Now complete the thought bubbles shown below, showing your ideas and how you arrived at them.

What has happened before?
What will happen next?
R

5. Share your ideas with the rest of the class. Which are the key pieces of evidence?

6. Now read the following extract from *Harry Potter and the Philosopher's Stone*. Harry has just discovered he is a magician. When Harry was a baby, an evil magician called Voldemort tried to kill him, but succeeded only in leaving a lightning scar on his forehead.
As you read, think about the information in this passage that is important for us to remember later in the story.

Harry took the wand and (feeling foolish) waved it around a bit, but Mr Ollivander snatched it out of his hand almost at once.

'Maple and phoenix feather. Seven inches. Quite whippy. Try –'

Harry tried – but he had hardly raised the wand when it, too, was snatched back by Mr Ollivander.

'No, no – here, ebony and unicorn hair, eight and a half inches, springy. Go on, go on, try it out.'

Harry tried. And tried. He had no idea what Mr Ollivander was waiting for. The pile of tried wands was mounting higher and higher on the spindly chair, but the more wands Mr Ollivander pulled from the shelves, the happier he seemed to become.

'Tricky customer, eh? Not to worry, we'll find the perfect match here somewhere – I wonder, now – yes, why not – unusual combination – holly and phoenix feather, eleven inches, nice and supple.'

Harry took the wand. He felt a sudden warmth in his fingers. He raised the wand above his head, brought it swishing down through the dusty air and a stream of red and gold sparks shot from the end like a firework, throwing dancing spots of light on to the walls. Hagrid whooped and clapped and Mr Ollivander cried, 'Oh, bravo! Yes, indeed, oh, very good. Well, well, well … how curious … how very curious …'

He put Harry's wand back into its box and wrapped it in brown paper, still muttering, 'Curious … curious …'

'Sorry,' said Harry,' but *what's* curious?'

Mr Ollivander fixed Harry with his pale stare.

'I remember every wand I've ever sold, Mr Potter. Every single wand. It so happens that the phoenix whose tail feather is in your wand, gave another feather – just one other. It is very curious indeed that you should be destined for this wand when its brother – why, its brother gave you that scar.'

From *Harry Potter and the Philosopher's Stone* by J. K. Rowling

1.4

7. Now jot down your ideas on a grid like the one below, suggesting why you think certain pieces of information are important for us to remember.

Extract from story	*Why this is important*	*What might happen later on?*
He raised the wand above his head, brought it swishing down through the dusty air and a stream of red and gold sparks shot from the end like a firework … *Hagrid whooped and clapped …* *'It is very curious indeed that you should be destined for this wand when its brother – why, its brother gave you that scar.'*		

Solution to key puzzle

- How do writers help their readers work at what has already happened in a story and predict what might be going to happen?

8. Draw up a list of what helped you to make guesses or predictions about what has already happened or might happen in the future.
9. What advice would you give to a reading detective who had to guess what happens later in the story?

10. Share your ideas with the rest of the class.

Now that you can use evidence to make predictions, the 'reading detective' trail is almost complete. Get ready for the final challenge!

1.4 The mystery unravelled

Key puzzle

- What skills do we use as readers to pick up vital clues, pieces of evidence and information to help us become true 'reading detectives'?

Remember!

- A **motive** is a reason for doing something.
- The **narrator's perspective** is how the storyteller presents information.
- To **infer** and **deduce** mean to 'read between the lines' in order to build a full picture.

Every picture tells a story

1. With a partner, study the picture carefully.
2. Note down what you think has happened immediately before. Then note down what made you think this.
3. Share your ideas with the rest of the class. Which elements of the picture were more useful than others in terms of building up a bigger picture?

Solve it, Sherlock

4. Read through the following short story. As you read, think carefully about the clues the writer leaves along the way.

'That was a neat program on UFO's,' said Nina to her cousin Max as they walked down the street. 'I think what really amazed me was that UFO's were reported as early as 1800.'

'That's pretty hard to believe,' said Max. 'Anyway, do you really believe there are such things?' Nina started to answer when they heard a loud scream coming from Coach Thornton's house.

'Come on,' shouted Max. They ran into the yard where the coach was staring at ten rose bushes that had been pulled from the ground.

'Look at that!' he demanded. 'Just look at that.'

'That's terrible,' cried Nina. 'Who could have done it?'

Coach Thornton looked disgusted. 'I had to bench three of my best football players for cutting class. They were pretty mad at me.'

'First thing, we'd better get these roses back in the ground,' said Max. 'Then we'll figure out who did it.'

Nina and Max helped Coach Thornton replant the roses. Then he invited them in for milk and cookies.

'Now,' said Nina. 'Am I right? You benched Sam Cartland, Mike Brooks, and Alex Avery.'

'And you lost the game,' added Max.

The coach rubbed his eyes. 'I know, but rules are rules.'

'I'll bet one of them did it to get even,' said Nina. 'How about we nose around a little?'

'Let's see,' said Max after they left. 'Coach said the roses were all right when he looked out at nine. But shortly after ten, he found them pulled up.'

'So we check to see who doesn't have an alibi between nine and ten. Look!' Nina pointed. 'There's Alex Avery over at the Dairy Bar.'

Alex looked up as they came in. 'Hi kids,' he drawled.

'Hello yourself,' said Max. 'We missed seeing you in the football game.'

'That was a bummer all right. But I guess the coach didn't have any choice.'

'Where you been all morning?' asked Nina.

'I've been right here since nine.' He turned to the girl behind the counter. 'Isn't that right, Amy?'

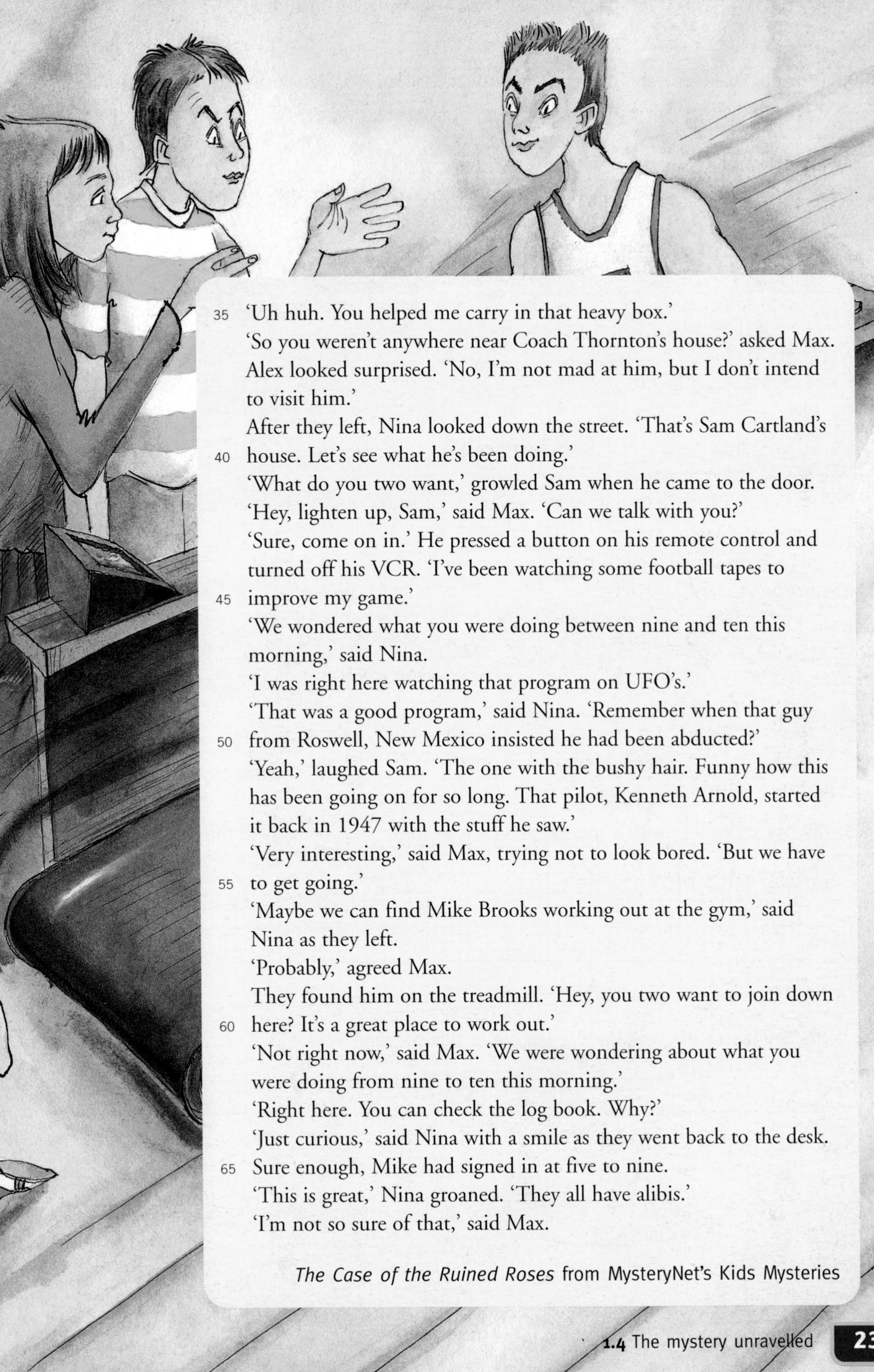

'Uh huh. You helped me carry in that heavy box.'

'So you weren't anywhere near Coach Thornton's house?' asked Max.

Alex looked surprised. 'No, I'm not mad at him, but I don't intend to visit him.'

After they left, Nina looked down the street. 'That's Sam Cartland's house. Let's see what he's been doing.'

'What do you two want,' growled Sam when he came to the door.

'Hey, lighten up, Sam,' said Max. 'Can we talk with you?'

'Sure, come on in.' He pressed a button on his remote control and turned off his VCR. 'I've been watching some football tapes to improve my game.'

'We wondered what you were doing between nine and ten this morning,' said Nina.

'I was right here watching that program on UFO's.'

'That was a good program,' said Nina. 'Remember when that guy from Roswell, New Mexico insisted he had been abducted?'

'Yeah,' laughed Sam. 'The one with the bushy hair. Funny how this has been going on for so long. That pilot, Kenneth Arnold, started it back in 1947 with the stuff he saw.'

'Very interesting,' said Max, trying not to look bored. 'But we have to get going.'

'Maybe we can find Mike Brooks working out at the gym,' said Nina as they left.

'Probably,' agreed Max.

They found him on the treadmill. 'Hey, you two want to join down here? It's a great place to work out.'

'Not right now,' said Max. 'We were wondering about what you were doing from nine to ten this morning.'

'Right here. You can check the log book. Why?'

'Just curious,' said Nina with a smile as they went back to the desk. Sure enough, Mike had signed in at five to nine.

'This is great,' Nina groaned. 'They all have alibis.'

'I'm not so sure of that,' said Max.

The Case of the Ruined Roses from MysteryNet's Kids Mysteries

1.5 **5.** Now think carefully about the three suspects. Fill in your detective's notebook showing whom you suspect and why.

Name of suspect	Motive	Alibi	Can alibi be 'backed-up'?	Are they your chief suspect?
Alex Avery				
Sam Cartland				
Mike Brooks				

6. Discuss your ideas with a partner and then write up your findings in the following way:

1.5 My chief suspect is ____________________ because ____________________

____

____

____.

The key pieces of evidence that led me to this decision were ____________________

____

____.

Solution to key puzzle

- What skills do we use as readers to pick up vital clues, pieces of evidence and information to help us become true 'reading detectives'?

1.6

7. With a partner, and looking back at the skills you have used in this unit, fill in the job description for a reading detective.

WANTED – READING DETECTIVE

Job will include: ______________________________

Essential qualities: ______________________________

Job prospects: ______________________________

Previous experience might include:

____

For further information please contact:

____

8. Display your reading detective descriptions in your classroom to remind you of the skills you have mastered and can use with all your English work.

Congratulations! Your mission is complete and you are now a fully qualified Reading Detective.

Let me entertain you!

This unit introduces you to the secret 'tricks of the trade' that make exciting and imaginative narratives. Once you've stored all of these in your writer's 'toolbox' you'll be ready to create your very own masterpieces for the writer's Hall of Fame.

2.1 Select your weapons

Key puzzles

- What 'tools' do writers use to ensure their work makes sense?
- What techniques do writers use to build variety into their work?

Remember!

- A **sentence** is a unit of language that makes sense on its own. When you write a sentence, make sure it begins with a capital letter and ends with a full stop, question mark or exclamation mark.
- Different punctuation marks at the end of sentences affect the way we say the sentence and the meaning that is conveyed.

A commanding voice

1. With a partner, read the sentences below. Decide which punctuation mark you would use at the end of each sentence to communicate the meaning effectively.

   Warning! With some of the sentences you could use several different punctuation marks, so you must be prepared to justify your ideas.

   - I don't believe it
   - Who says fashion is silly
   - Did you see that goal
   - How old are you
   - I can't do it
   - The party was brilliant

2. Now share your ideas with the rest of the class, reading out the sentences according to the punctuation you have chosen.

Use your weapons wisely

2.1

3. Look at the passage below. You will notice that all the sentences end with the same punctuation mark: a full stop.

Read through the passage carefully, then see if you can make it sound more interesting by replacing some of the full stops with different punctuation marks. Don't forget, however, that you can have too much of a good thing. Overusing question marks and exclamation marks can put the reader off, so make sure you use them wisely.

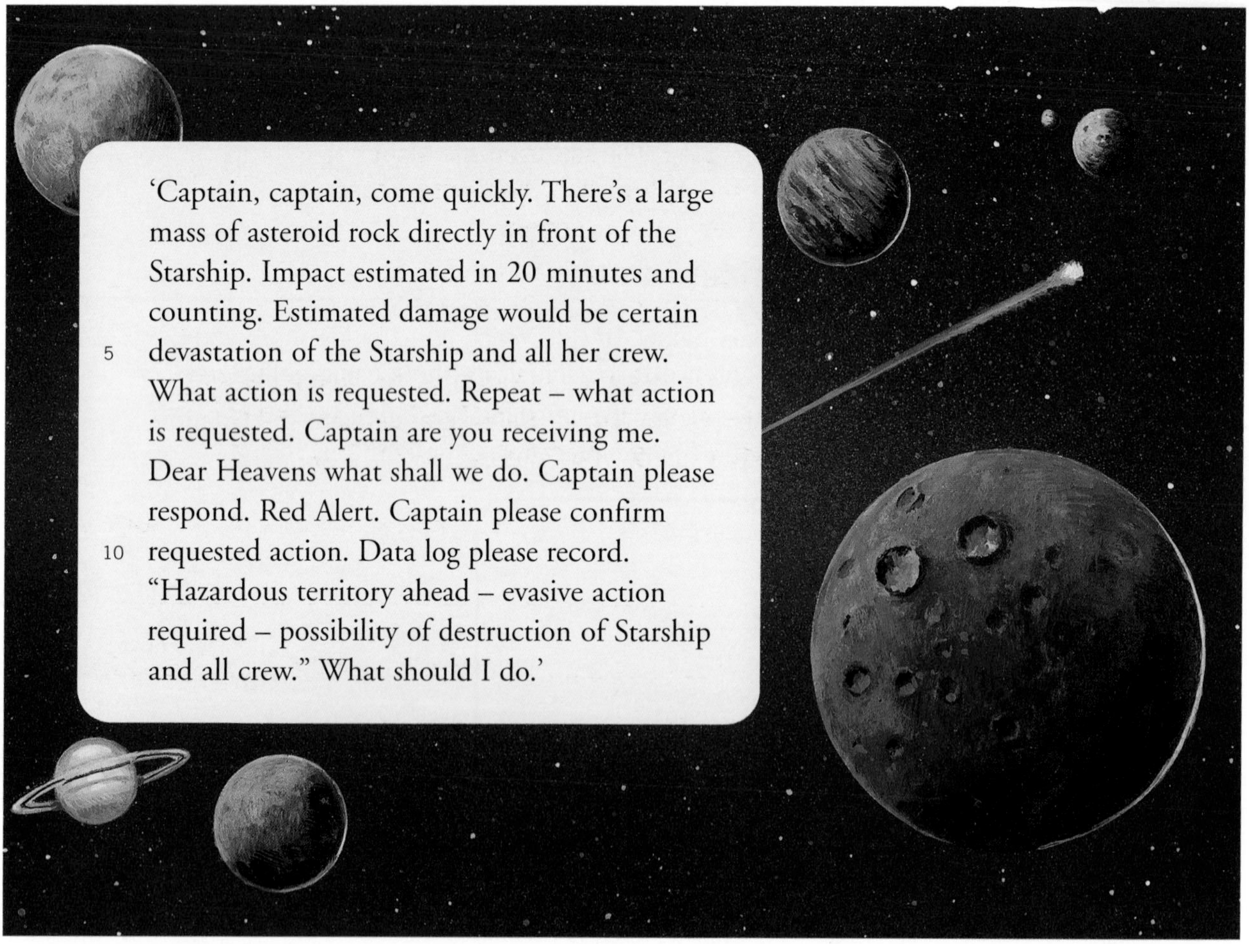

'Captain, captain, come quickly. There's a large mass of asteroid rock directly in front of the Starship. Impact estimated in 20 minutes and counting. Estimated damage would be certain devastation of the Starship and all her crew. What action is requested. Repeat – what action is requested. Captain are you receiving me. Dear Heavens what shall we do. Captain please respond. Red Alert. Captain please confirm requested action. Data log please record. "Hazardous territory ahead – evasive action required – possibility of destruction of Starship and all crew." What should I do.'

4. Feed back your ideas to the rest of the class. Which sentences did you *all* agree needed either a question mark or an exclamation mark?

The right punctuation in the right place helps the reader understand how the writer wanted the passage to be read. It also helps to make your writing sound lively and interesting.

You can also enhance your writing by varying the structure of your sentences and by adding extra details in particular ways.

One of the ways you can expand a piece of writing is by adding a **subordinate clause** to some of your sentences.

In any sentence there is a **main clause**. This is the part of the sentence that makes sense on its own without any other information, e.g. I ran to the controls.

A subordinate clause does not make sense on its own and ***depends*** on the main clause in a sentence to communicate its meaning. It adds information on how, when, where and why something happens, e.g. I ran to the controls ***as fast as I could***. We still need the main clause to make the sentence make sense, but the subordinate clause gives us extra information on *how* I ran to the controls.

We can also move the subordinate clause around to make our writing more varied, e.g. ***As fast as I could***, I ran to the controls.

5. Now look at the sentences below and see if you can complete them by adding subordinate clauses in the spaces. Remember to think **how?** (quickly, slowly, cautiously, angrily ...), **when? where? why?** (because, although, if ...).

   a) ______________________________, the captain checked his watch.

   b) The guard sounded the alert, ______________________________.

   c) The attack, ______________________, was the largest they had met so far.

   d) The captain, ______________________________, did not respond.

   e) ______________________________, a red alert was sounded.

We can often adapt this idea of moving information around a sentence by starting sentences with verbs ending in -ing, e.g:

Walking away from the control panel ...
Screaming for his life ...
Shouting in case anyone could hear ...

6. Now read the passage below. A young writer is trying to create an exciting and tense scene for a new space fantasy story. However, their writing is a little unimaginative and needs some adaptations and added detail to capture the reader's interest. Using what you know about how a piece sounds (**tone**) and variety in sentences, adapt the piece to make it more appealing to a reader.

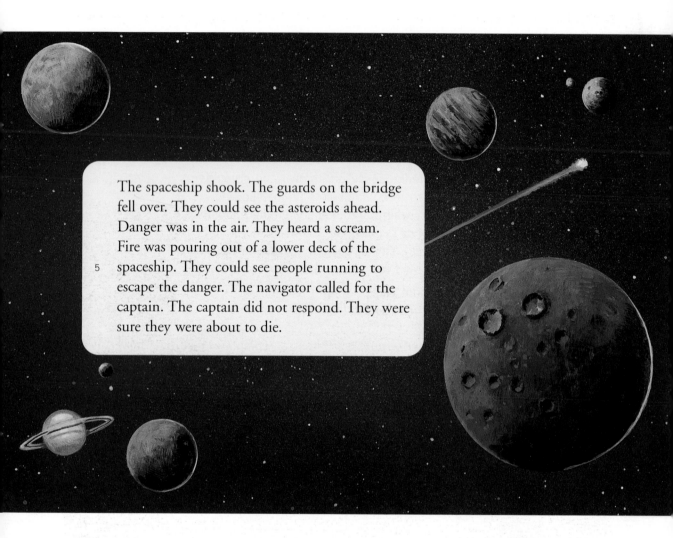

The spaceship shook. The guards on the bridge fell over. They could see the asteroids ahead. Danger was in the air. They heard a scream. Fire was pouring out of a lower deck of the spaceship. They could see people running to escape the danger. The navigator called for the captain. The captain did not respond. They were sure they were about to die.

Solution to key puzzles

- What 'tools' do writers use to ensure their work makes sense?
- What techniques do writers use to build variety into their work?

2.1

7. You have been asked to write back to the author of the unimaginative space passage, offering three top tips on how they can improve their writing.

   With a partner, decide what you are going to say to this writer, making sure you put your most important point first. You also need to remember that you might need to explain some technical terms and give examples.

8. Share your ideas with the rest of the class. Which pieces of advice were most popular? As a class, which technique would you rate as the chart topper?

2.2 Heroes and villains

Key puzzle

- How can a writer make descriptions of characters interesting and engaging?

Remember!

- **Nouns** are names of things, people, places or feelings, e.g. witch.
- **Adjectives** are descriptive words we put with nouns to paint a more detailed picture, e.g. wicked.
- **Verbs** are words that express actions, e.g. flying, or states of being, e.g. is.
- **Adverbs** are descriptive words that tell us how an action is carried out, e.g. quickly.

Thou art a villain

1. With a partner, make a list of all the villains you can think of from stories, TV and films.
2. Now look at the images below. Make a list of all the adjectives you can think of that would describe these characters.

3. Now look back at your list of villains. How many of your words can be used to describe *your* villains?
4. What do the villains on your list have in common in the way they look, the powers they have, or the clothes they wear?

First impressions count

5. Read the three descriptions below of characters from well-known children's books. Each of these descriptions comes from the first time we meet the character in the story.

> The thin man stepped out of the cauldron, staring at Harry … and Harry stared back into the face that had haunted his nightmares for three years. Whiter than a skull, with wide, livid scarlet eyes, and a nose that was as flat as a snake's, with slits for nostrils …
> Lord Voldemort had risen again.
>
> From *Harry Potter and the Goblet of Fire* by J. K. Rowling

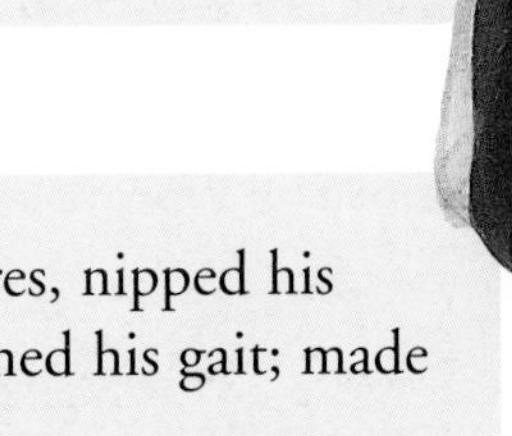

> The cold within him froze his old features, nipped his pointed nose, shrivelled his cheek, stiffened his gait; made his eyes red, his thin lips blue …
>
> From *A Christmas Carol* by Charles Dickens

> … on a much higher seat in the middle of the sledge sat a very different person – a great lady, taller than any woman that Edmund had ever seen. She also was covered in white fur up to her throat and held a long straight golden wand in her right hand and wore a golden crown on her head. Her face was white – not merely pale, but white like snow or paper or icing-sugar, except for her very red mouth. It was a beautiful face in other respects, but proud and cold and stern.
>
> From *The Lion, the Witch and the Wardrobe* by C. S. Lewis

6. Which words and phrases in these extracts convey a sense of evil?

7. Which of the descriptions do you think gives us the best understanding of the type of person that character is? Use a frame like the one on page 34 to help you organise your answer.

Elements of description	What it suggests to me
Harry Potter and the Goblet of Fire	
A Christmas Carol *the cold within him*	*Suggests he had a cold, mean character*
The Lion, the Witch and the Wardrobe	

2.3

8. Now look again at the description of the White Witch from *The Lion, the Witch and the Wardrobe*. There are parts of this description that could be used for a 'good' or nice character in a story.

Look at the passage below. Some of the words that could lead to different interpretations have been taken out. With a partner, discuss which words and phrases you could place in each gap. Then rewrite the passage to make the White Witch sound completely sinister.

> On a much higher seat in the middle of the sledge sat a very ____________ person – a ____________ lady, taller than any woman that Edmund had ever seen. She also was covered in white fur up to her throat and held a ____________________ in her right hand and wore a ____________ on her head. Her face was ____________ , but ____________ like ____________ , except for her very ____________ mouth. It was a beautiful face in other respects, but ________________________ .

2.3

9. Now, thinking about how these writers have created a sense of evil, use some of their ideas to write your own brief description of a villain for your own narrative.

Solution to key puzzle

- How can a writer make descriptions of characters interesting and engaging?

10. When you have written the description of your own villain, take a different coloured pen and make notes around the description. Show where you have used particular words and phrases to create the right effect.

11. Now swap with a partner, read their comments and suggest how they might improve the description of their villain.

2.3 Imagine a place where ...

Key puzzle

- How does a writer create atmospheric and realistic settings?

Remember!

- **Nouns** are names of things, people, places or feelings, e.g. forest.
- **Adjectives** are descriptive words we put with nouns to paint a more detailed picture, e.g. spooky.
- A **noun phrase** is a collection of words that includes a noun which helps to paint a much more detailed picture, e.g. the small, decaying, haunted cottage.

Untangle the strings

1. Look at the list of adjectives below. They were all suggested during a brainstorm to describe a haunted cottage in the woods. If you were describing such a place, which words would you choose? Discuss this with a partner; decide which words you would discard and make a list of the words you would use.

• spooky	• dark	• lonely	• crumbling
• creaky	• little	• frightening	• large
• looming	• bleak	• imposing	• sinister
• creepy	• cobwebbed	• forgotten	• deserted

2. Look at the noun phrase in the box below. The adjectives were chosen by one student to describe the haunted cottage. This student has tried a bit too hard to be descriptive, and instead of creating an effective noun phrase, they have created a long, rambling list.
Trim the list of adjectives to create an effective noun phrase to describe the haunted cottage.

> The sinister, creepy, cobwebbed, imposing, spooky, decaying cottage

3. Feedback your ideas to the rest of the class. What key points should we remember when creating effective descriptions?

Let your senses guide you

An effective part of describing things is to say what you can see, and also to describe what you hear, smell, touch and taste.

4. Read the extracts below and on the next page, noting which senses the authors appeal to, in order to create effective descriptions of the settings.

This was obviously the kitchen. Huge cold black kitchen range, and a battered electric cooker that must have been 1950s. Stone-flagged floor, with beetles scurrying away into the dark corners. The sink was full of dirty dishes, on to which the cold tap dripped, its sound quarrelling with the ticking of the clock that had followed him in. Every work-surface was covered with an intricate clutter, like a spider's web to catch the eye.

From *Woman and Home* by Robert Westall

There were old chests of drawers and broken wash-basins and bags of cement, ancient doors leaning against the walls, deck chairs with the cloth seats rotted away. Great rolls of rope and cable hung from nails. Heaps of water pipes and great boxes of rusty nails were scattered on the floor. Everything was covered in dust and spiders' webs. There was mortar that had fallen from the walls. There was a little window in one of the walls but it was filthy and there were rolls of cracked lino standing in front of it. The place stank of rot and dust. Even the bricks were crumbling like they couldn't bear the weight any more. It was like the whole thing was sick of itself and would collapse in a heap and have to get bulldozed away.

From *Skellig* by David Almond

But by then all of us could hear the sound of falling water, cool and clear; and irresistible even to Arnie. We ducked under the branches and picked our way along the bank of the stream, which soon became a clear, dark little river. I had my sandals, with the heel straps undone, so I wasn't too badly off, except that my knee was hurting. Arnie and Miranda managed somehow, with Arnie complaining all the time. It was a relief to be out of the sun, but as tropical jungles go, this wasn't a very attractive example. We didn't see any flowers. A few tall trees with thick rusty-brown trunks loomed up into the sky, but mostly the vegetation was thorny bushes, thorny creepers and giant grassblades that cut our hands when we pushed them aside. We heard birds, and once something (probably a big monkey) went crashing through the branches over our heads.

From *Dr Franklin's Island* by Ann Halam

2.4

5. With a partner, take one of the extracts above and fill in a grid like the one below, noting examples of the various senses the author appeals to.

Name of extract	Sight	Sound	Smell	Touch	Taste

2.4

6. Now, think of a place that you would like to describe. This might be a castle, a forest, a house, a beach, an attic – and fill in a grid like the one below, with adjectives that cover more than one sense.

Place	Sight	Sound	Smell	Touch	Taste

2.4

7. Now write a paragraph describing your setting. Use what you know about noun phrases, and appeal to a variety of senses. Remember, you need to paint as vivid a picture as possible so that the reader can really imagine the place.

Solution to key puzzle

- How does a writer create atmospheric and realistic settings?

8. With a partner, take turns to describe different places. Use a range of different descriptive techniques, e.g. *This place is dark, sinister and scary.* Your partner has to guess what place you are describing.

9. Look at the three statements below. Number them 1–3 (1 = the most important thing to remember when writing descriptions; 3 = the least important). Be prepared to give reasons for your answers.

   a) You need to include noun phrases in a really good piece of description.

   b) You need to have lots of adjectives in a really good piece of description.

   c) You need to appeal to all the senses in a really good piece of good description.

2.4 Prepare for impact

Key puzzle

- How does a writer build up and maintain tension and suspense in a piece of writing?

Remember!

- **First person** is when we write as 'I'.
- **Third person** is when we write he/she/they.
- **A sentence** should have a **subject** (who or what the sentence is about) a **verb** (action or being word) and an **object** (who or what the subject affects). However, some authors break this pattern for effect.

Bend it, shape it – elastic writing

1. Look at the three sentences below. With a partner, adapt them to create more tension, mystery and impact. You may shorten them, re-structure them or even change some of the words to do this.

   a) He looked up and saw the fierce beast, mouth wide open and eyes blazing in front of him, ready to attack.

   b) The door slammed shut and he suddenly realised he was very frightened of the dark, remembering his childhood nightmares.

   c) The cliff edge was getting nearer and nearer and she felt her foot slip and the gravel began to drop down the deep ravine.

2. Feed back your sentences to other members of the class. What different strategies have people used to adapt the sentences? Which do you think are the most effective?

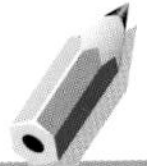

We have impact

When you were rewriting the sentences, you may have kept sentences very short, repeated ideas or started a sentence in an unexpected way.

2.5

3. Read the two extracts below and, with a partner, note what different effects the author is using to make an impact on the reader.

Here's a good rule to remember about rattlesnakes and scorpions: If you don't bother them, they won't bother you.

Usually.

Being bitten by a scorpion or even a rattlesnake is not the worst thing that can happen to you. You won't die.

Usually.

Sometimes a camper will try to be bitten by a scorpion, or even a small rattlesnake. Then he will get to spend a day or two recovering in his tent, instead of having to dig a hole out on the lake.

But you don't want to be bitten by a yellow-spotted lizard. That's the worst thing that can happen to you. You will die a slow and painful death.

Always.

From *Holes* by Louis Sachar

The wizard grew older before their eyes. He sank down upon his chair, his face lined and grey.

'It is the stone. It is the stone. No other has that heart of fire. And it was by me, and I did not hear it call.'

He sat, his eyes clouded, a tired, world-weary, old man.

Then wrath kindled in him, and spread like flame. He sprang from his chair with all the vigour of youth, and he seemed to grow in stature, and his presence filled the cave.

From *The Weirdstone of Brisingamen* by Alan Garner

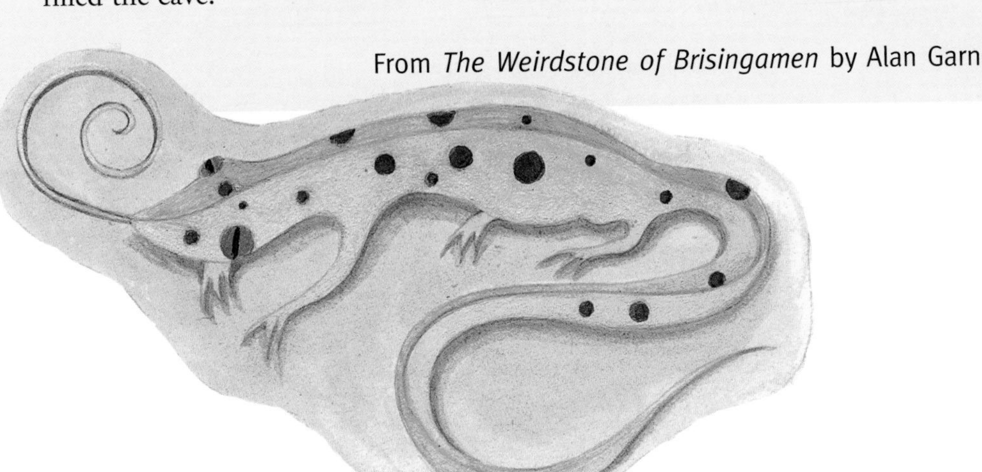

4. As a class, make a list of the techniques you have spotted that help to make an impact on the reader.

Another technique that authors sometimes use is to write as if they are the central character (in the first person – 'I'). Then they take us through the events step by step with a succession of short sentences, e.g.:

I was standing at the edge of the forest. I heard an owl screech. I turned and something brushed my face.

5. Imagine you are the central character in a ghost story. You have wandered away from your friends and now find yourself in a deserted graveyard. Write a paragraph, in the first person (I), and try to build up the tension of the situation with a range of short sentences and other techniques we have spotted, like repetition.
6. Now swap your paragraph with a partner. In a different colour, make notes around their writing, picking out the key features that build up the tension.

Pulling it all together

7. Look back at the descriptions of a villain and a setting that you wrote earlier in this unit. Use your skills to create a moment of tension and impact including either your villain or your setting (or even both!). Describe a moment of crisis and drama that will have your readers on the edge of their seats and biting their nails!

Solution to key puzzle

- How does a writer build up and maintain tension and suspense in a piece of writing?

8. **Top writers' checklist** A famous magazine has asked you to write a checklist for authors. Your list must include all the techniques they need to use if they are to be successful. With a partner, look back at all the skills you have learned or revisited in this unit and put together your own 'Essential writing toolbox list' for new writers.

9. As a class, choose the best list and display it to help you with other pieces of writing.

Congratulations! Now you've stored all of these techniques in your writer's 'toolbox' you are ready to create your very own masterpieces for all to read and enjoy!

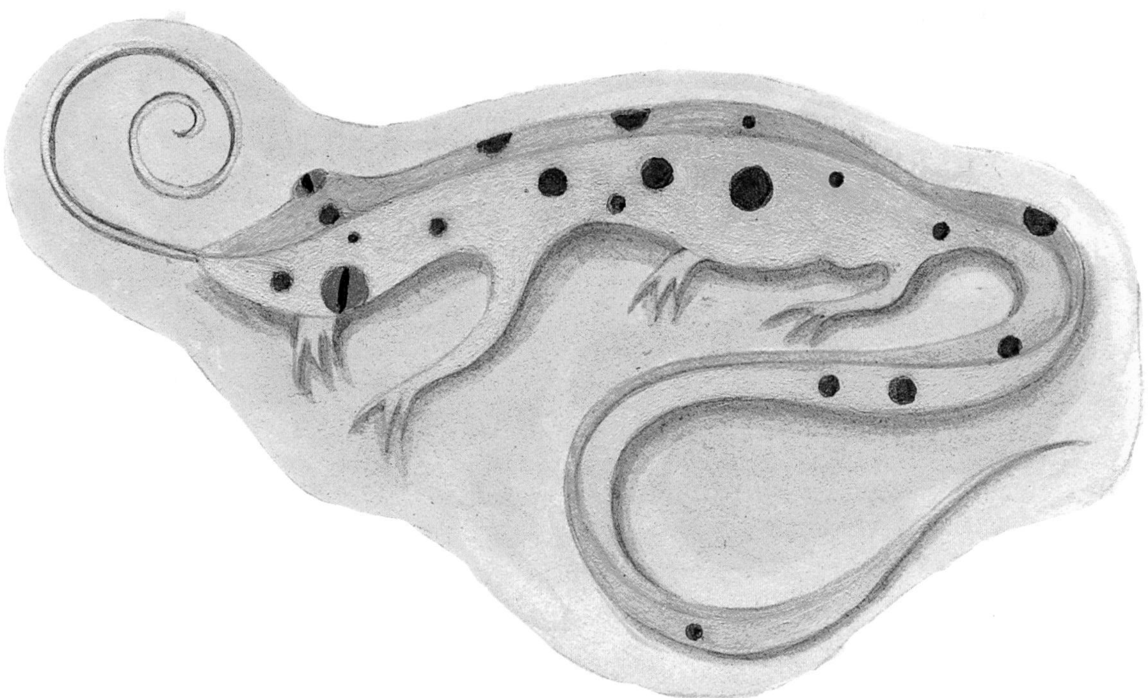

Read all about it – the facts and the fiction

There are lots of non-fiction texts waiting to be read in this unit. When you've read them, you are challenged to sort out the facts from the fiction, and show off your note-making skills.

Are you ready to become a research wizard? Read on ...

3.1 What I really need to know

Key puzzle

- When we read a piece of text, what strategies can help us to focus on the issues we need to make a note of?

Remember!

- **Information retrieval** is finding out what we want to know, using different sources.
- A **source** is a text that offers information.
- **Selecting** is making choices.
- **Relevance** is where we select the information we need to know.

Fact or fiction?

1. With a partner, brainstorm ideas on the differences between information texts and fiction. Think about content, style, layout and why people read the two kinds of text.

2. Share your ideas with the rest of the class. As a class, decide on an ending to the following statement:

   In English we read non-fiction/information texts to …

   Display this where the whole class can see it. It will remind you to use the skills you will learn about and practise in this unit.

Magical information

3. Read the following extract. The writer offers information on the origins of some of the creatures in the Harry Potter books. In this extract, he is providing links between pixies and the house elves that help Harry in his adventures.

What Is the Favourite Trick of Cornish Pixies?

Pixies are energetic household spirits from the legends of Cornwall and the south-west of England. Most stories depict them dressed in green, wearing a pointed cap. They have youthful faces and many have red hair. J. K. Rowling departs from tradition in *Harry Potter and the Chamber of Secrets* and *Fantastic Beasts and Where to Find Them*, describing them as 'electric blue and about eight inches high'.

In folklore, pixies are often said to act like the house elves of Harry's world. They can be quite helpful but will disappear if given a gift of clothes. Unlike house elves, who are happy to do all the work, pixies will nip at lazy members of a household.

Pixies love to dance under the moonlight. At times they also take horses from stalls and ride them all night, returning them exhausted – and with mysteriously knotted manes – in the morning. But their favourite activity is to lead travellers astray. People who have lost their way (or are in any way bewildered or confused) are said to be 'pixie-led'. This disorienting spell may be broken by taking off one's jacket and putting it on again, inside out.

From *The Magical Worlds of Harry Potter* by David Colbert

3.1 **4.** Read the extract again, and note down five key points the author makes about pixies.

5. Now you have your five points, discuss them with a partner and agree on your joint final five points.

6. Look again at the points you have chosen. Using a 1–5 scale, where 1 is the *most important*, list your points in order of importance.

   Use a grid like the one below and make sure that you give a reason for why you have placed the piece of information where you have in the list.

3.1

Piece of information (most important first)	Reasons for position in list
1	
2	
3	
4	
5	

7. Now look again at the extract. You have had to leave out pieces of information from your selected list. With your partner, select the three pieces of information you think are least important and place them in a grid like the one below, where 1 is the *least important* point.

3.1

Piece of information (least important first)	Reasons for position in list
1	
2	
3	

You should now have the piece of information you think is most important and the piece of information you think is least important.

8. Share your ideas with the rest of the class, justifying your ideas. Your challenge is to come up with a class list of the five most important points and the three least important points.

When you read information texts, it is important that you don't write down everything. You have to select the most important things – the things you really need to know.

Solution to key puzzle

- When we read a piece of text, what strategies can help us to focus on the issues we need to make a note of?

9. Think about how many times you read the passage. Also think about how you decided which points were important and which were not so important.

   Design a five-point checklist for your partner on how to read a piece of information and pick out the main points.

10. Swap ideas with your partner and make a note of the points to help you in your work.

3.2 A page full of detail

Key puzzle

- How do words and pictures in an information text combine to offer the reader a range of information?

Remember!

- **Layout** is the arrangement of words and pictures on the page.
- **Headings** and **sub-headings** are usually larger than the rest of the text; they stand out to show us where a new section starts.

Name the sections

1. With a partner, brainstorm all the different features you might find in a newspaper article – for example, different kinds of headings, eyewitness statements.
2. Now think about a web page. What different features might you find there? For example, different sections, weblinks.
3. What are the similarities and differences between the two?

Headline

Subheading

Opening paragraph gives key facts – what, who, where, when etc

caption – tells us about picture

Subheading
more information about story and can include interviews etc

Subheading
text text text text text text text text text text text text text text text text text text text text text text text text text text text text text text text text

Subheading
text text text text text text text text text text text text text text text text text text text text text text text text text text text text text text text text text text text text text text text text text text text text text text text text

text text text text text text text text text text text text text text text text text text text text text text text text text text text text text text text text text text text text text text text text text text text text text text text text text text text text text text text text text text text text text text text text text text text text text text text text

A page full of news

4. Look at The **News***paper* web page on page 51. Make sure you look at the whole page as well as reading the main story.
Remember, web pages aren't always checked carefully. So, you may find mistakes or untruths – or made-up stories presented as fact!

5. What kind of audience do you think this page is aimed at? Try to find as many reasons as possible to support your answer.

6. What ideas about the story does the photo give?

7. What do the subheadings do in this story? What key ideas do they give us?

3.2 8. The article gives us some facts about tracking devices, and also some opinions/interviews. Note down the key facts, and in the next column the opinions, with the people who are quoted.

Facts the article tells us	*Opinions/peopled interviewed*
The chip is 2cm long	*Kevin Warwick, Professor of Cybernetics - says parents and children are scared*

9. The article gives us some information about dangers and fears for children and parents. What links could be added to the page to give more information? E.g:

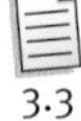

3.3

- Advice for children about safety
- Advice for worried parents
- Advice about safety for children using chatrooms

What would you like to see a link to?

Solution to key puzzle

10. Working with a partner, plan and sketch out a web page giving advice about 'stranger danger' for parents and children

You will need to plan:

- What you will include on the page and why
- The layout, including:
  - Headlines and main article, using subheadings to help the reader through the story
  - Pictures
  - Links to other useful sites (you could make these up or research them for yourself)
  - Discussion/chatrooms of the subject

Nervous

Is tracking the answer?

Abuse happens in the home

Harmed

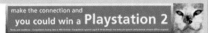

TheNews*paper*

Take me to _

Wednesday 18 November 2002

Letts EDUCATIONAL

Is tracking the answer?

Kevin Warwick, Professor of Cybernetics at Reading University, is facing a queue of parents asking for their children to be fitted with this microchip traking device. 'My phone is going berserk,' he says. 'There are a lot of scared parents and children out there.'

The 2cm-long chip will cost £20 and is put into a child's arm by a doctor under a local anaesthetic. It works by sending out radio waves that can be picked up by a mobile phone linked to a computer. The child then can be traced anywhere and at any time.

Normally the chip is in sleep mode and gives out a signal only when the mobile phone network sends in the wake-up code.

Nervous

First in line for chipping is Danielle Duval, age 11, from Reading in Berkshire. She hopes to be fitted with the device within the next few weeks. Although Danielle is nervous about the operation, she is very keen to be tagged. 'It is better than getting kidnapped,' she says. 'Most of my friends would have it too.'

Harmed

But not everyone likes the idea. Mary MacLeod of the National Family and Parenting Institute says: 'Knowing where the child is does not mean that the child is safe. The truth is that children are more likely to be harmed by someone they know than by a stranger.'

The National Society for the Prevention of Cruelty to Children agrees. A spokesman says: 'Parents must always remember that child abductions are extremely rare.'

Abuse happens in the home

Bernard Allbrecht, an electronics expert based in London, has other concerns. He is determined to get Professor Warwick stopped. He says: 'There could be a case for assault if their operation goes ahead, so I spoke to the police, but didn't have any luck. They felt that if parents gave consent it would be all right, but I believe there are wider legal principles involved here.'

If getting chipped is too much for teens with anxious parents, My Child Tracker software for mobile phones may be a better choice. At the touch of a locate button, a parent can pin-point their teenager on a map on their mobile screen. However, the system works only so long as both mobiles are switched on.

To Tag or not to Tag? What do YOU think? E-mail stagging@thenewspaper.org.uk or write to Tagging, The Newspaper, P.O. Box 121, Tunbridge, Kent TN12 5ZR

3.3 *Skipping across the page*

Key puzzle

- How can we gain information from a text without having to read every word closely?

Remember!

- **Scanning** is looking quickly through the text to pick out and locate key words.
- **Skimming** is looking rapidly through the text to gain a general impression of the text.
- **Captions** are words of explanation that go with pictures, diagrams or photographs.
- An **image** is a picture or a photograph.

Reading under pressure

1. If you had to find some information very quickly, where might you look?

   With a partner, make a list of the most useful places.
2. Feedback your ideas to the rest of the class. Which three areas were mentioned most?
3. Now imagine you have found your information and have only five minutes to read a whole page and make some notes ready to feedback information to a group.

   What strategies might you use to help you complete the task?
4. Again, feedback your ideas to the rest of the class and make a class list of the ways other people help themselves to cope with lots of text when they have limited time.

On your marks, get set, read!

5. Look at the TV page below. What time is *Final Score* on? What can I watch if I want to watch something after 9 p.m.?

BBC1

7.00 CBeebies starting with Spot's Musical Adventures. (R) (S) (C) 7.10 The Shiny Show. (S) (C) 7.30 CBBC starting with Pocket Dragon Adventures. (R) (S) (C) 7.45 UBOS. (R) (S) (C) 8.10 The Wild Thornberrys. (R) (S) (C) 8.35 Rugrats. (R) (S) (C) 9.00 The Saturday Show. (S) (C) 12.00 BBC News; Weather. (C)

12.10 Football Focus: Ray Stubbs and Mark Lawrenson preview the start of a new Premiership season.
1.00 Grandstand. (S)
4.45 Final Score.
5.25 BBC News, Weather. (C)
5.40 Regional News; Weather
5.45 Big Break. (S) (C)
6.15 Sizzling Bloomers. (R) (S) (C)
6.55 The Weakest Link Special: Fashion. (S) (C)
7.45 The National Lottery: Winning Lines. Phillip Schofield presents. (S) (C)
8.30 Judge John Deed. Feature-length drama starring Martin Shaw as a maverick High Court judge caught in a conflict of personal and professional interests when his daughter is arrested during a demonstration. (R) (S) (C)
10.00 BBC News; Regional News and Weather; (C) National Lottery Update
10.20 Jim Davidson: On The Edge: Stand-up comedy with the funnyman. Last in series. (S) (C)
11.00 FILM: Parenthood (1989): Family comedy. Steve Martin stars. (S) (C)
1.00 Patrick Kielty Almost Live. (R) (S) (C)
1.35 It's Only TV But I Like It. (R) (S) (C) Weatherview
2.10 Top of the Pops. (R) (S) (C)
2.40 BBC News 24

CHANNEL 4

6.00 Grabbit the Rabbit. (R) (T) 6.10 The Hoobs. (R) (T) 6.35 The Hoobs. (R) (T) 7.00 GT on 4. (T) 7.30 Honda Formula 4-Stroke Powerboating Championship. (T) 8.00 Trans World Sport. (T) 9.00 The Morning Line. 10.00 Cricket Roadshow. 11.00 World Rally: Shakedown. (T) 11.30 British Rally Championship. (T) 12.00 Little House on the Prairie. (R) (T) 1.00 Little House on the Prairie. (R) (T) 2.00 Channel 4 at the races: From Newbury, Newmarket and Ripon. Featuring the 4.10 Stan James Geoffrey Freer Stakes. (T). **4.25 Extinct. (R) (T) 4.55 FILM: Tora! Tora! Tora!** (1970): Based on the Battle of Pearl Harbor. Martin Balsam stars. (T)

7.30 Channel 4 News. (T)
7.55 A Very British Revolution: British farmers' protests in September 2000. (T).
9.30 FILM: Cruel Intentions (1999): Drama updating the premise of *Dangerous Liaisons*, focusing on a spoilt rich girl who bets her stepbrother he can't seduce an innocent virgin. Sarah Michelle Gellar stars, with Ryan Phillippe and Reese Witherspoon. (T)

11.20 Angel. (T). 12.20 The FilmFour Prize for Short Film. 1.20 FILM: The Spanish Prisoner (1998): Drama, starring Campbell Scott. (T) **3.20 FILM: The Verdict** (1982): Courtroom drama, starring Paul Newman. **5.30 Countdown. (R) (S) (T)**

6. Now think about the way you looked at the listings page.
Did you read each channel line by line?
What did you do?
Try to explain what your eyes were doing to find the right information.

7. Now look quickly at the recipe below to pick out the key points. You only have 30 seconds.

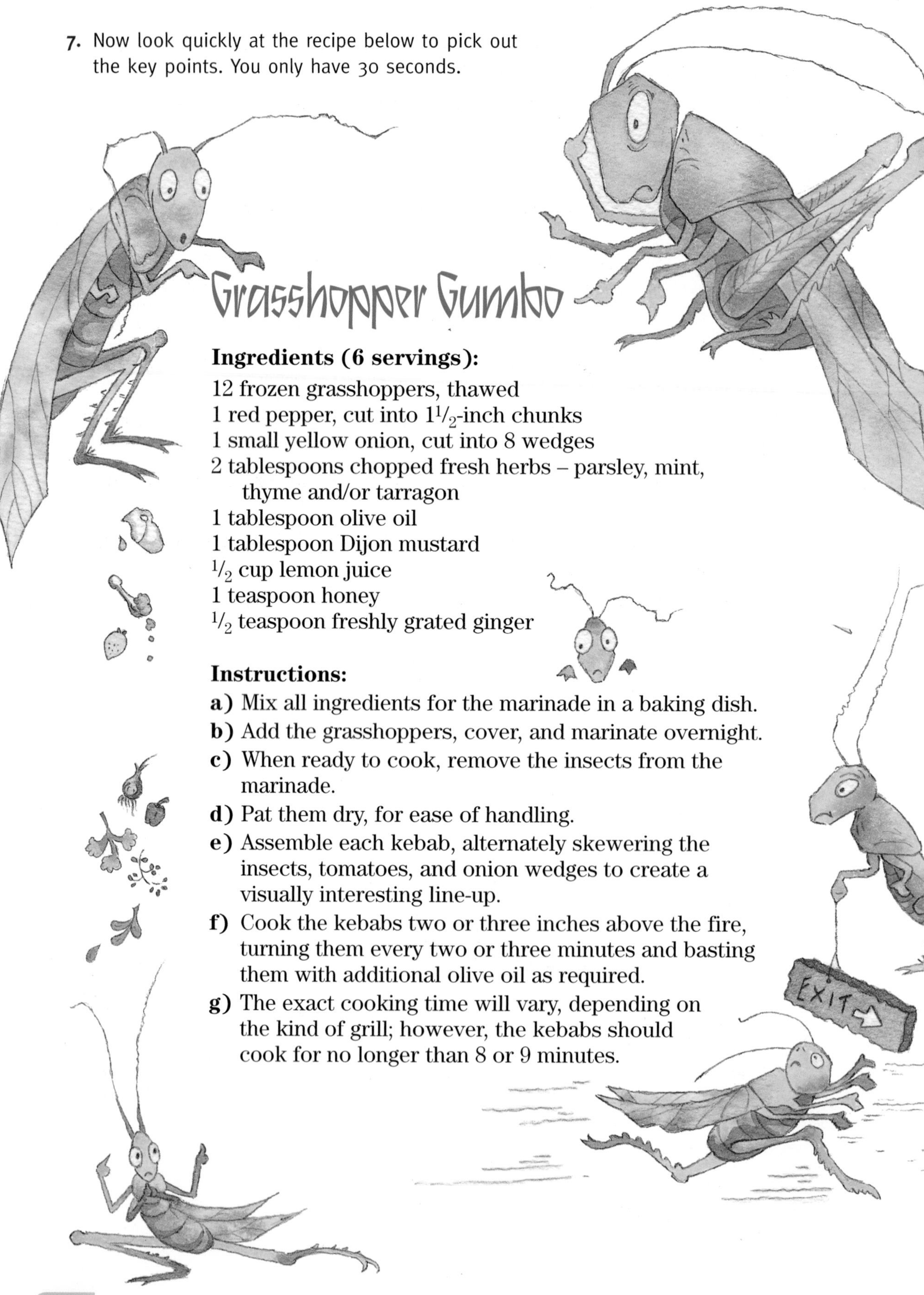

Grasshopper Gumbo

Ingredients (6 servings):

12 frozen grasshoppers, thawed
1 red pepper, cut into $1^1/_2$-inch chunks
1 small yellow onion, cut into 8 wedges
2 tablespoons chopped fresh herbs – parsley, mint, thyme and/or tarragon
1 tablespoon olive oil
1 tablespoon Dijon mustard
$^1/_2$ cup lemon juice
1 teaspoon honey
$^1/_2$ teaspoon freshly grated ginger

Instructions:

a) Mix all ingredients for the marinade in a baking dish.
b) Add the grasshoppers, cover, and marinate overnight.
c) When ready to cook, remove the insects from the marinade.
d) Pat them dry, for ease of handling.
e) Assemble each kebab, alternately skewering the insects, tomatoes, and onion wedges to create a visually interesting line-up.
f) Cook the kebabs two or three inches above the fire, turning them every two or three minutes and basting them with additional olive oil as required.
g) The exact cooking time will vary, depending on the kind of grill; however, the kebabs should cook for no longer than 8 or 9 minutes.

8. Now, cover up the recipe. Jot down the main ingredients and preparation/cooking stages that the recipe asks you to go through.

9. Think about the way you looked at the recipe when you knew you only had 30 seconds.
   Did you read every word?
   What did you do?
   Try to explain what your eyes were doing to get a general overview of the recipe.

To do these two activities you probably used skimming and scanning skills. These are essential when searching for information in a large amount of text and in a limited time span.

10. Now, with a partner, read the two articles on page 56, from the *Horrible Histories* series.

3.4 11. Thinking about skimming and scanning skills, devise three questions for each article
3.5 that test either:

   - scanning skills – where you look quickly through the text to pick out and locate key words, or
   - skimming skills – where you look rapidly through the text to gain a general impression of it.

Don't forget to think about images and captions too.

SPORTS SPECIAL

GREECE IN GAMES DISPUTE

NUDE ATHLETES CONFUSED

580BC

The Pan-Hellenic games are in turmoil. Ever since 776 BC sportsmen have been meeting in Olympia at four-year intervals to see who's the best. The Olympic Games have become such a part of Greek culture that everybody takes a month or two off fighting to give their men the chance to compete.

All over the Greek-speaking world, from the Black Sea to Italy, athletes have made the effort to be there.

But now there's competition. Three other cities are muscling in on the act. 'This is a very serious business,' said an Olympic spokesman. 'The Olympic games have always set the standard. For example, ever since Orsippos's pants fell down in 720 BC and he lost the race, all athletes have competed in the buff. We've defined every single event, from long jump to discus. But now these others are trying to copy us. It's disgraceful.'

CORNER

But the new games-hosts are holding their own.

'We resent the way Olympia is trying to corner the market,' one Corinth senator told the *Gazette*. 'We reckon that if they're going to hold games every four years that leaves three years free for us, Delphi and Nemea to stage our own events.'

Each city has the backing of a top deity. Olympia and Nemea have Zeus, Delphi has Apollo and Corinth has Poseidon. So if any athlete asks 'Who's going to hold it?' we say 'it's in the hands of the Gods'!

'GET OUT OF MY HEAD!'

Keyhole surgeon faces lockup

1179

Keyhole surgery? Angry patient Eldred Turnip is giving surgeons the length of his tongue. Having checked in for a trepanning operation – a routine procedure which involves drilling a hole in the skull to relieve headaches or bouts of madness – he came out with a gaping cavity the size of a saucer.

Latest thing

'They told me keyhole surgery was the latest thing,' he told the Messenger. 'But frankly I may as well have had it done by the local gravedigger. I mean, look at it.'

Turnip is calling for revenge. 'Six years in a dank dungeon would do,' he told us.

Unfortunately for Eldred, although seers and sages predict that keys and keyholes will get smaller in the future, they're still extremely large and rather clumsy devices. Medical experts say Eldred should have avoided new-fangled hands-on surgery and stuck to the tried and trusted route of medicines and magic charms.

Mallet

'These so-called surgeons are just jumped-up barbers, or battlefield medics,' said top physician Lancelot de Lozenge, 'and expecting them to perform intricate operations is like asking a road-builder to fix your delicate gold bracelet with a great big mallet. Medicine has so much to offer I can't understand why Eldred took such drastic action.'

Hands-on

Lozenge went on to tell the Messenger, 'Therapeutic flowers and plants are available in great numbers, as are such health-giving foods as sugar and treacle. Why fix a bad head with painful surgery when a lotion of ginger and cinnamon will do the trick with much less fuss. Best of all get yourself touched by someone with healing powers. Kings are best, if you can get near enough to beg them to touch you, but a Jew or Muslim who has converted to Christianity also has the ability to cure all sorts of maladies by simply laying their hands on the patient.'

Wrong signs

'Besides, these surgeons often perform their grisly chores at completely inappropriate times of the year. Anyone connected with medicine knows that you can only treat particular ailments at set astrological moments. I, for example, would only tend to a patient with bad headaches when the Moon is rising in Sagittarius. It's just asking for trouble to do it at any other time.'

Solution to key puzzle

- How can we gain information from a text without having to read every word closely?

12. Finally, swap your questions with another pair. Challenge them to find the answers to your questions faster than you can find the answers to their questions.

3.4 Looking from all points of view

Key puzzle

- How do we select the most useful information for a particular task?

Remember!

- A **fact** is a detail we can prove.
- **Interpretation** is our own understanding of what a text means.
- **Summarising** is giving a brief outline of the information we have read.
- **Perspective** is a point of view.

Different slants

3.6

1. Look carefully at the image below.

2. What do you think has happened?
3. How can you tell that the adult and the child have different views/feelings about it? What clues are there in the picture?
4. With a partner, try to describe the situation from the adult's point of view, and then from the child's.

This shows us how we can look at the same information in different ways and for different purposes. We are suggesting different interpretations of what the people involved might think.

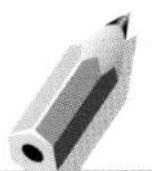

Select, reject and justify

3.7

5. Read the extract below, about the Second World War.

Grotty Gas Masks

The British people were worried that Hitler would use poisoned gas against the British cities. So everyone in Britain was given a gas mask, a horribly smelly rubber mask with little glass windows that soon steamed up. The bottom of the mask filled up with saliva and sweat. The silly cardboard boxes fell apart within a week; many children ended up carrying their gas masks over the shoulder on the end of a dog lead.

Gruesome Gas Facts

1. There were 'gas detectors' placed at street corners. These were supposed to light up if gas was in the air. They were never used. There was never ever a gas bomb attack on Britain … yet some people reckon gas masks were one of the great successes of the war! Why? Because Adolf Hitler knew about the gas masks. He knew it would be a waste of time to bomb people with gas when the people were so well prepared – so he didn't bother!
2. Someone invented a gas-proof pram so you could take baby for a walk. It looked a bit like a coffin on wheels with a little chimney to let in gas-free air.
3. The masks made good carriers for children's bottles of school ink or the odd packet of sweets … fine, until they had an emergency gas mask practice.
4. Gas masks were usually carried in their cardboard boxes. But, if you had some spare money, you could go to a shop and buy a smart carrier made of fancy material. Shops started selling ladies' handbags with special pouches for the gas mask.
5. Men with beards had a real problem with gas masks. One woman managed to fit her husband's head into a gas mask by rolling his beard up with curling pins. But the Cistercian monks, who always wore beards, had no curling pins. They had to shave their beards off.
6. Children were persuaded to wear their masks by making them into 'fun masks'. One of the most common was the red and blue 'Mickey Mouse' mask. Children also discovered that if they wore the mask and blew very hard, the air rushed out of the side and made a very rude noise. The punishment for doing this in school was usually a whack with a cane!

From *The Blitzed Brits* by Terry Deary

6. What do you think are the three most important points about gas masks in this article?

7. Which three points about gas masks do you think would appeal most to children?

3.8

8. Now look at all the points listed in the extract. Using a grid like the one below, list the points in order of interest to:
   - children
   - teachers
   - someone writing about children in wartime.

Points likely to interest children	*Reasons*

Points likely to interest teachers	*Reasons*

Points likely to interest writer, about children in wartime	*Reasons*

9. Feedback your ideas and reasons to the rest of the class.

10. As a class, choose one of the groups (children, teachers or writers) and say which ideas are the most interesting and the least interesting. Remember to give reasons for your answers.

11. Now, in no more than five sentences, pick out the main facts about gas masks from the passage. Write them down in a way that is brief and easy to understand. Do not include unnecessary detail.

Solution to key puzzle

- How do we select the most useful information for a particular task?

12. With a partner, devise four statements explaining how we might set about selecting the most relevant information from a text.

13. Now write two statements that give poor advice on how to select the most important information from a text.

14. Swap your statements with another pair and divide them in two columns: good advice and bad advice.

Congratulations! You have now proved you can tell facts from fiction, the important from the unimportant. You can skim and scan too. You are now a fully fledged research wizard!

All aboard for a magical mystery tour

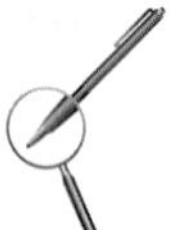

This unit takes you on a whistle-stop tour of detailed descriptions, impressive information texts and excellent explanations. You will need to use all your observation skills to help you spot the differences between different types of writing. Once you've worked it out, you will use all your descriptive and organisational skills to write your very own tour guide.

So hold on tight ... we're off to explore!

4.1 *Ready, steady, instruct ...*

Key puzzle

- What do writers need to remember when they are writing instructions for someone on how to complete a particular task?

That's the way to do it!

1. Look at the instructions below on how to create a cartoon monster. Note down the key words that make sure we sketch the monster in the right order.

Remember!

- **Instructions** direct or teach someone how to do something clearly and in an ordered way.
- **Time sequence markers** are words that give us an idea of time, such as *first, when, then, next, soon, immediately, after a few seconds.* They are often called temporal connectives.

Here's how to create your own instant baddy. Magnificently monsterish! First, draw two eyeballs and a lumpy nose … add a mouthful of rotten teeth … next, draw the shape of the head … and then the final, creepy details … Warts and spots on the nose and chin … rings round the eyes … hair coming out of ears and nostrils … and cute little brown and green blotches on the yellow teeth.

From *Count Drawcula's Cartoon Fun* by Frank Rodgers

Although the instructions tell us how to draw the monster step by step, we could add more instructions to make the monster easier to draw.

2. With a partner, devise another three steps that would make the process clearer, e.g. information about the shape of the mouth, or the size and shape of the ears.
3. Now try out your full set of instructions on another pair to see if you have improved the explanation of how to create a cartoon monster.

Lesson recipes

We are surrounded by instructions every day: recipes, food packets, DIY leaflets, 'How to play the game' instructions and many more.

4. With a partner, think of the different types of instructions you have read recently. Make a list of the things these instructions have in common, e.g.: equipment list; the order to do things in; how to ..., use of the second person (you should).
5. Now read the extract below. You are going to create instructions for a Victorian school pupil from what you learn.

Who'd want to be a Victorian Schoolchild?

If you were a schoolchild in Victorian England, you would have found school very different from schools of today!

If you were learning to write you'd have to make sure you followed the teacher's instructions carefully or you would find yourself on the receiving end of some harsh words or even worse - the cane!

A writing lesson would usually last for about half an hour and it was essential that you had a straight ruler, a sharpened pencil, a pen and a 'copybook' for you to write in. You would find ink for your pen in the ink well set into your desk. However, when you started to write you would have had to have been very careful as you would discover that the pen had a very scratchy, leaky nib. You would have been asked to copy sentences from the blackboard over and over again and if your work was not neat enough you would have missed your play time and would have to start all over again!

4.1

6. Now, using the extract on the previous page and a grid like the one below, adapt the information about Victorian lessons to create a set of instructions for a Victorian school pupil.

How to survive and succeed in the Victorian classroom	
Equipment needed	*Skills/abilities needed* *E.g. Good memory*
Instructions *1.* *2.* *3.* *4.* *etc.*	

Useful words and phrases
Copybook, Straight Ruler, Sharpened Pencil, Pen, Ink well, nib.
First, next, after that, finally.

Solution to key puzzle

- What do writers need to remember when they are writing instructions for someone on how to complete a particular task?

7. Study the anagrams below. Each one is a key feature in the successful writing of instructions. With a partner, see if you can beat the clock and work each one out.

- itme qenucees rarmkse
- eaetdldi sriucinontts
- tequeipmn sitl
- eracl misa

4.2 An eye for detail

Key puzzle

- What skills are essential when we want to describe people and places in a limited number of words?

Remember!

- **Description** is writing that makes the behaviour or appearance of someone or something clear to the reader.

Unravel the riddle

1. The riddle below describes a famous landmark. Can you guess what it is?

> My first letter is also a drink.
> My middle word is a capital.
> I can offer you a good view and a fairground-type ride.
> My last word is watching you.

2. Now, with a partner, try to devise your own quick riddle to try out on others. Remember, it can be a place or a person.

Riddles like these get us to focus only on the most important aspects of a person or place.

Now read on and see other ways of using our descriptive powers to paint a picture in the reader's mind.

Fact files

3. Look carefully at the two fact file clippings below. Why do you think the two clippings have different sub-headings? What sub-headings would you use for creating a fact file on
   a) a teacher
   b) a pupil at your school?
4. Imagine you have to interview these two characters. You have been given these fact files as background information to read first. Note down the questions you would ask the characters during your interviews. (What points do we want more detail about?)
5. Now share your ideas with the rest of the class. What questions would most of the class want to ask?

MARIO

Occupation
Plumber

Nationality
Italian

Favourite Hobby
Coin collecting

Wears
Blue overalls, red top, red hat and won't be seen without his moustache

Companions
Princess Toadstool, Yoshi

Secret to success
Mama's lasagne

LARA CROFT

Occupation
Tomb raider (explorer, adventurer)

Nationality
British

Accomplishments
Uncovering Atlantean pyramid
Killed Bigfoot in North America.

Lives
In a Mansion in Surrey

Miscellaneous
Her father is a Lord

Fact files are generally produced to provide key information on people and characters, but they can also to make us want to find out more.

6. Now study the two fact files below carefully. Notice that they have different headings. ('Nick says' is a comment from the creator of Wallace and Gromit.)

Wallace & Gromit - Wallace

http://www.aardman.com/wallaceandgromit/homesweethome/wallace/index.shtml

Wallace's Home Page

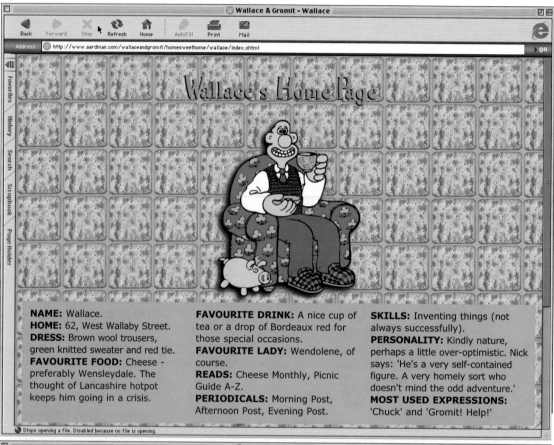

NAME: Wallace.
HOME: 62, West Wallaby Street.
DRESS: Brown wool trousers, green knitted sweater and red tie.
FAVOURITE FOOD: Cheese - preferably Wensleydale. The thought of Lancashire hotpot keeps him going in a crisis.
FAVOURITE DRINK: A nice cup of tea or a drop of Bordeaux red for those special occasions.
FAVOURITE LADY: Wendolene, of course.
READS: Cheese Monthly, Picnic Guide A-Z.
PERIODICALS: Morning Post, Afternoon Post, Evening Post.
SKILLS: Inventing things (not always successfully).
PERSONALITY: Kindly nature, perhaps a little over-optimistic. Nick says: 'He's a very self-contained figure. A very homely sort who doesn't mind the odd adventure.'
MOST USED EXPRESSIONS: 'Chuck' and 'Gromit! Help!'

Stops opening a file. Disabled because no file is opening.

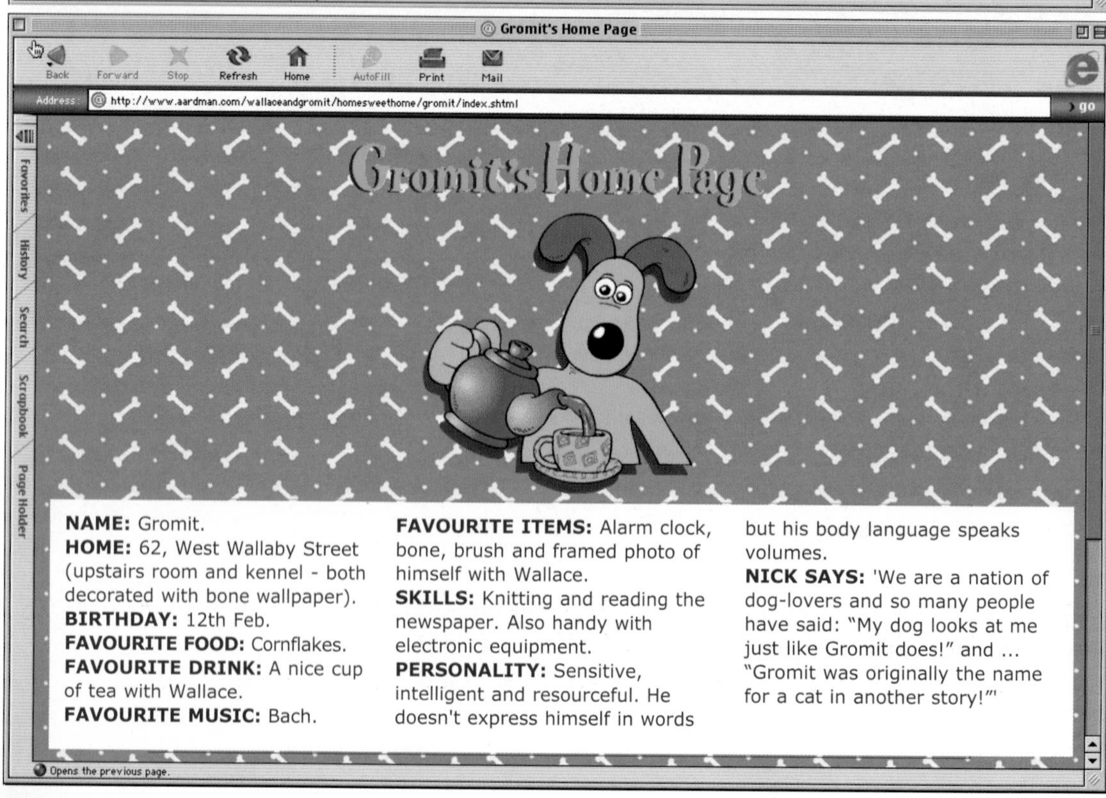

Gromit's Home Page

http://www.aardman.com/wallaceandgromit/homesweethome/gromit/index.shtml

Gromit's Home Page

NAME: Gromit.
HOME: 62, West Wallaby Street (upstairs room and kennel - both decorated with bone wallpaper).
BIRTHDAY: 12th Feb.
FAVOURITE FOOD: Cornflakes.
FAVOURITE DRINK: A nice cup of tea with Wallace.
FAVOURITE MUSIC: Bach.
FAVOURITE ITEMS: Alarm clock, bone, brush and framed photo of himself with Wallace.
SKILLS: Knitting and reading the newspaper. Also handy with electronic equipment.
PERSONALITY: Sensitive, intelligent and resourceful. He doesn't express himself in words but his body language speaks volumes.
NICK SAYS: 'We are a nation of dog-lovers and so many people have said: "My dog looks at me just like Gromit does!" and ... "Gromit was originally the name for a cat in another story!"'

Opens the previous page.

7. Look at all the different headings in the two fact files. If you had to write a fact file on yourself, what headings would you choose to include apart from the **Name** heading?

8. Now think about what a close friend or a member of your family might include in a fact file about you. Remember, they might want to give different information from the information you would choose to include. What headings do you think they would have in your fact file?

4.2

9. Imagine you are one of your friends or a family member who has been asked to write a fact file about you. Create it from their point of view (perspective). Remember, they may include information you would rather they didn't. Use a grid like the one below to help you.

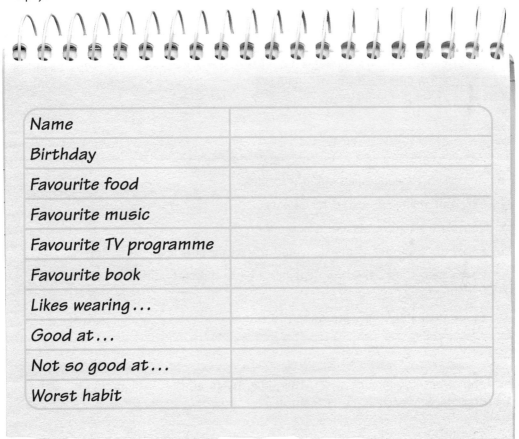

Name	
Birthday	
Favourite food	
Favourite music	
Favourite TV programme	
Favourite book	
Likes wearing...	
Good at...	
Not so good at...	
Worst habit	

Solution to key puzzle

- What skills are essential when we want to describe people and places in a limited number of words?

10. Now, with a partner, devise a 'Top Tips' leaflet that shows the top five things a writer needs to remember to write a really effective fact file.

Share your ideas with the rest of the class and display them as reminders.

4.3 Tantalising tours

Key puzzle

- What different language styles do we use when writing tour guides and leaflets?

Remember!

- An **explanation** is written to explain how or why something happens.
- **Persuasion** is when we try to convince others.
- **Tone** is the sound of a piece of writing.

Chocs away!

4.3

1. Study the picture of the chocolate factory on the page opposite. Then look at the explanations of the different processes below, and try to match them with the different sections of the factory.

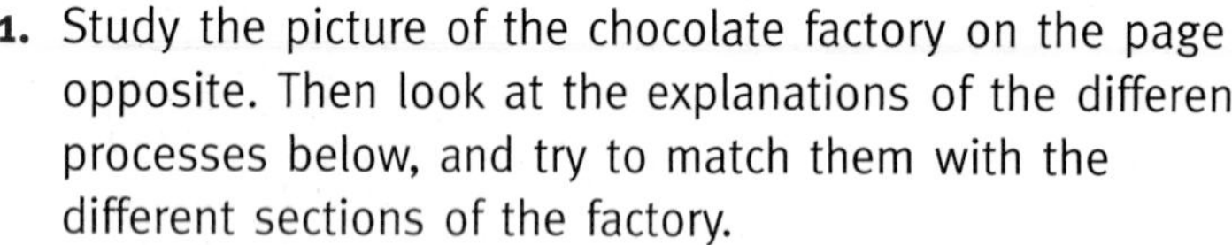

a) Processed chocolate is shaped into bars.
b) Milk and sugar are tested for quality.
c) Chocolate bars are placed in cooling machine.
d) Sacks of cocoa beans are delivered to factory floor using a pulley.
e) Cocoa beans are baked and crushed before they are added to any other ingredients.
f) Cocoa beans and milk are added to the mixer.

2. Now look at each statement again. This time, try to add an explanation to each one to give a reason why each stage is there, e.g.:

   Chocolate bars are placed in cooling machine **because they need to be solid before a wrapper can be placed around them.**

3. Share your explanations with the rest of the class. Which words did you find yourself using most often to help you add a reason to each statement?

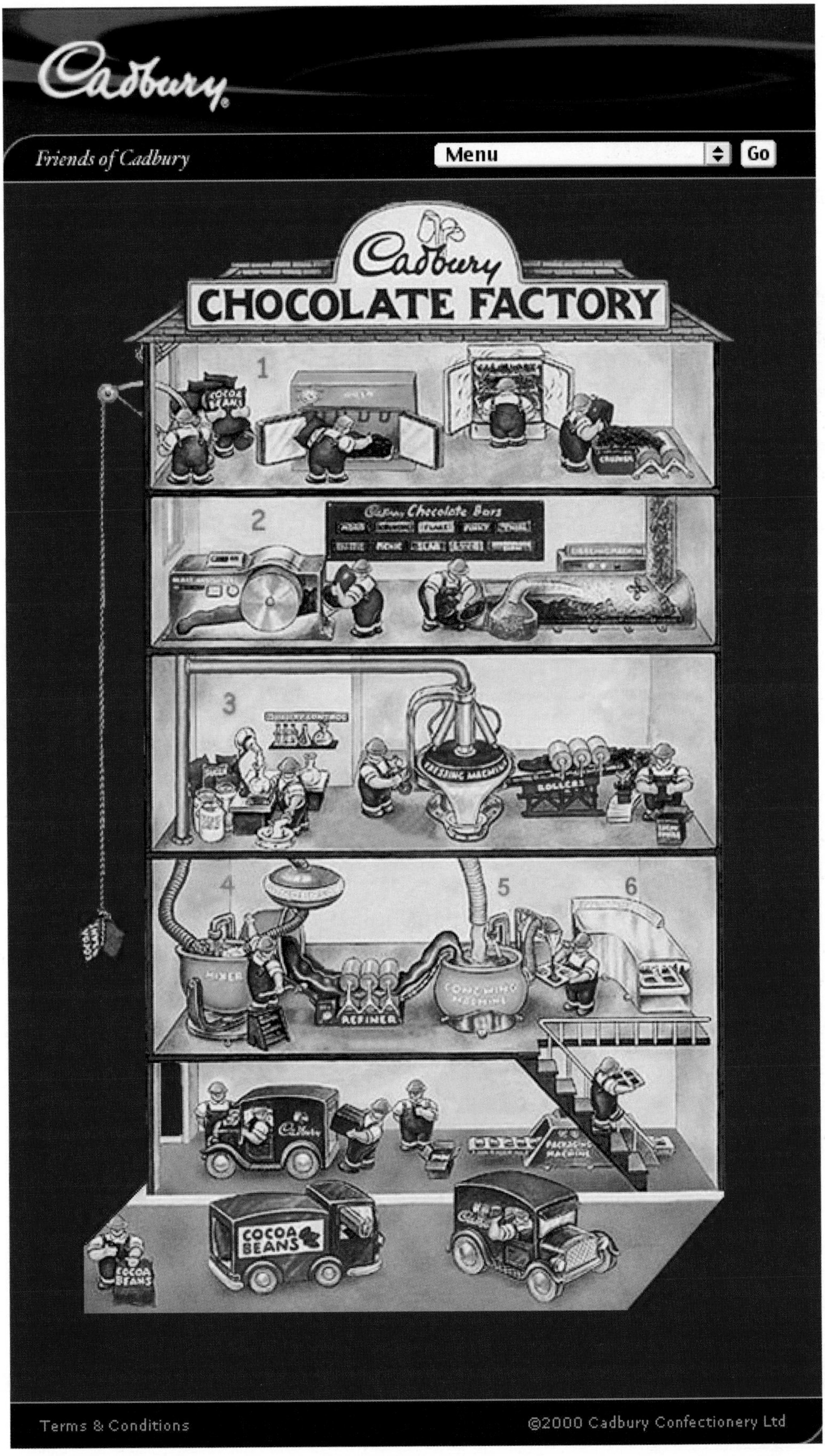

Friends of Cadbury

Menu | Go

Cadbury
CHOCOLATE FACTORY

1

2

Cadbury Chocolate Bars

3

4 5 6

MIXER

REFINER

CONCHING MACHINE

COCOA BEANS

Terms & Conditions

Perfect persuasion

When writing a leaflet or an information guide to a place, a writer has to make sure they describe and explain what is on offer. They also have to try to persuade the reader to visit the place.

4. Read the information guide below. It describes a new chocolate factory opening in New Zealand.

Opening July 2002

Cadbury World – a sensation in sight, smell and sound. Visitors will view their favourite chocolate products being made, experience the mystique of a working chocolate factory, sample and purchase special products and much more.

Cadbury World is located in the centre of Dunedin City at the Cadbury factory site. We offer the opportunity to tour our Visitors Centre and view many heritage and interactive displays. Learn about the history of chocolate and Cadbury in New Zealand and some of the secrets/tricks for handling and cooking with chocolate.

This will be followed by a guided tour of our factory where visitors will see many of their favourite products being made and guides will not only explain the process but will also share interesting stories and quirky snippets of our history, process and about chocolate in general. The Factory Tour is also supported by visual and interactive displays. Tour duration will be 40–45 minutes.

On completion of the Factory Tour, visitors are invited to visit the Cadbury World retail store where they can purchase special products and merchandise. The store offers visitors the chance to create their own product. The aim of this is to have our guests take away something special and personalised as well as a great memory of their experience at Cadbury World.

Tours will run 7 days a week between the hours of 9am–4pm (this can be tailored to suit).

4.4

5. Now draw a grid like the one below and fill it in. Pick out and explain the words and phrases from the information guide that you think are particularly persuasive. There is an example to start you off.

Persuasive words and phrases	Why this is persuasive
Sensation in sight, smell and sound	It appeals to more than one of the senses and makes the reader think of 'taste' too.

4.5

6. Now, using the information from this guide, select the most important details and put together a fact file using headings like the ones below.

Tour of Cadbury World

What is Cadbury World?
Where is Cadbury World?
What does a visit to Cadbury World include?
What special features appeal to children?

Remember to select only the most important details about the tourist attraction. Your fact file needs only to convey the facts, not advertise the attraction.

Solution to key puzzle

- What different language styles do we use when writing tour guides and leaflets?

7. Swap your fact file with a partner. What differences in content and tone are there between your fact file and the information guide?

8. As a class, draw up an 'Essentials' list of all the things you need to include in a good information leaflet. This will help you in your next task ...

4.4 Exciting expeditions

Key puzzle

- What differences are there between descriptions of places in stories and description of places in tour guides and leaflets?

Remember!

- **Persuasion** is when we try to convince others.
- **Tone** is the sound of a piece of writing.

Chocolate guides galore

1. Read the extract below.

They were looking down upon a lovely valley. There were green meadows on either side of the valley, and along the bottom of it there flowed a great brown river.

What is more, there was a tremendous waterfall halfway along the river – a steep cliff over which the water curled and rolled in a solid sheet, and then went crashing down into a boiling churning whirlpool of froth and spray.

Below the waterfall (and this was the most astonishing sight of all), a whole mass of enormous glass pipes were dangling down into the river from somewhere high up in the ceiling! They really were *enormous*, those pipes. There must have been a dozen of them at least, and they were sucking up the brownish muddy water from the river and carrying it away to goodness knows where. And because they were made of glass, you could see the liquid flowing and bubbling along inside them, and above the noise of the waterfall, you could hear the never-ending suck-suck-sucking sound of the pipes as they did their work …

'*There!*' cried Mr Wonka, dancing up and down and pointing his gold-topped cane at the great brown river. 'It's *all* chocolate! Every drop of that river is hot melted chocolate of the finest quality.'

From *Charlie and the Chocolate Factory* by Roald Dahl

2. With a partner, make a list of the details from this extract you would include if you were writing a tour guide for visitors to Mr Wonka's factory.
3. Which details would you not include? Why?
4. Compile a class list of the essential points. You will be able to refer back to this list later in the unit.

The tour must go on

5. Now read the following extracts, also from *Charlie and the Chocolate Factory*. As you read, note how many different things Charlie and Grandpa Joe see on the tour and the kind of things that are going on inside the Inventing Room.

The Inventing Room

Charlie Bucket stared around the gigantic room in which he now found himself. The place was like a witch's kitchen! All about him black metal pots were boiling and bubbling on huge stoves, and kettles were hissing and pans were sizzling, and strange iron machines were clanking and spluttering, and there were pipes running all over the ceiling and walls, and the whole place was filled with smoke and steam and delicious rich smells.

The Tour

Grandpa Joe and Charlie were half running and half walking to keep up with Mr Wonka, but they were able to read what it said on quite a few of the doors as they hurried by.
EATABLE MARSHMALLOW PILLOWS, it said on one …
LICKABLE WALLPAPER FOR NURSERIES, it said on the next door …
HOT ICE CREAMS FOR COLD DAYS, it said on the next door …
COWS THAT GIVE CHOCOLATE MILK, it said on the next door …
FIZZY LIFTING DRINKS, it said on the next door …
SQUARE SWEETS THAT LOOK ROUND

From *Charlie and the Chocolate Factory* by Roald Dahl

6. Now, with a partner, fill in a grid like the one below. Note the kind of things you might need to point out to visitors in a tour guide to Mr Wonka's factory.

4.6

If there is no description of what is happening in a particular room, you will have to use your imagination! Make up an interesting detail to explain to visitors how the different sweets, drinks and ice creams are created.

Place	Essential information for guide
THE CHOCOLATE VALLEY	• *A valley within the chocolate factory where a river of chocolate runs through the middle.* • *A waterfall of chocolate makes a spectacular sight.* • *All the chocolate from the river is carried away by glass pipes to other rooms in the factory.*
THE INVENTING ROOM	
EATABLE MARSHMALLOW PILLOWS	
LICKABLE WALLPAPER FOR NURSERIES	
HOT ICE CREAMS FOR COLD DAYS	
COWS THAT GIVE CHOCOLATE MILK	
FIZZY LIFTING DRINKS	
SQUARE SWEETS THAT LOOK ROUND	

Now that we have all the information for our tour guide leaflet, we need to think about how we put it together and the kind of language we should use.

7. Below is a list of things that other tourist attractions include in their tour guide leaflets. With a partner, discuss which of these things would be the most important to include in your tour guide leaflet about Mr Wonka's factory.

- A map showing how to get there.
- A map of the tourist attraction itself, with points of interest numbered.
- Admission prices.
- A history of the attraction.
- Information on the most important rooms/places/attractions, including: what it is, why it is special, what visitors might gain from visiting it.
- An actual tour with a 'Start from here' point and a trail that takes visitors through all the rooms or areas.
- Pictures/photographs of key points of interest.

8. Feed back your ideas to the rest of the class. Explain why you have chosen these elements for your leaflet.

Tour guide leaflets are often used to advertise places of interest. This means that it is important that they are well presented and written in a way that will make people want to visit.

9. Look at the tour guide leaflet on the next page. As a class, discuss which are the most important elements of this leaflet and which elements you would want to recreate in your own leaflet.

10. Now, using all the information collected so far, design your own tour guide leaflet for a 'Magical Mystery Tour of Mr Wonka's Chocolate Factory'.

THE MAGICAL KINGDOM OF CAMELOT THEME PARK

THE GAUNTLET

LANCASHIRE'S FAMILY ATTRACTION OF THE YEAR 2002

Use of pictures

Persuasive language
(makes it sound magical)
spooky special celebration

Use of different fonts
Save £9 by order of the KING!

Subheadings
MAGICAL BIRTHDAY PARTIES

Headings
Now the weather can't spoil YOUR FUN!

Use of capitals
HALF PRICE RETURN TICKET

KING'S REALM
1 CASTLE ENTERTAINMENT CENTRE
The Jousting Knights dodgems, the amazing Towers of Fun playland and the latest arcade games - all under cover inside our incredible family entertainment centre.
2 CATS OF THE ROUND TABLE
Don't miss our amazing animatronic show and discover a day in the life of a knight.
3 CATERPILLAR CAPERS
Perfect for the little ones, this junior rollercoaster is always a favourite.
4 CAMELOT LOG FLUME
It's thrills and spills all the way on this super splashing water ride!
5 PENDRAGON'S PLUNGE
Take the whole family slip-sliding down three breathtaking water chutes - and don't forget the photo!
6 FORMULA-K GO-KARTS
Enjoy lap after lap of high speed thrills on this super karting circuit (extra charge).
KNIGHT'S VALLEY
7 KING ARTHUR'S CASTLE
Take your seat for two of Camelot's fun-filled shows, starring Merlin the Magician and the juggling jester, Mad Edgar (see back cover for details).
8 DRAGON FLYER
Tamed by the Knights of Camelot, this noble beast will give you a spectacular view of our kingdom.
9 THE GALLEON
To and fro you'll go as you really get in the swing of things on this perilous pirate ship!
10 AVALON JOUSTING ARENA
Whatever you do, don't miss this spectacular display of courage and horsemanship in the only permanent open air jousting arena in the country with seating under cover (see back for details).
11 KINGDOM IN THE CLOUDS
Sit back, relax and enjoy the view as you take to the skies.
12 GAMES SQUARE
Roll up, roll up for all the fun of the fair - try your luck at the ring toss, wiggle wire and much, much more.
13 GAMES SQUARE ARCADE
A host of slot machines and video games.
Squire Bumpkin's FRIENDLY FARM
THE GAUNTLET
The RACK
millions MAZE
CASTLE ENTERTAINMENT CENTRE
SOFT PLAY
DODGEMS
Jousting Knights
ARCADE GAMES
Cats OF THE ROUND TABLE
ENTRANCE
Camelot gifts are always a big hit!
FOOD COURT
WIMPY
DOUWE EGBERTS
GAMES SQUARE
JOUSTING ARENA
HOSPITALITY VENUE
THEATRE MAD EDGAR & MERLIN SHOWS
Wherever you go in Camelot, you won't go hungry!
CAR PARK 7
CAR PARK 5
CAR PARK 6
CAR PARK 4
ANTIQUES FAIR EVERY SUNDAY
PARK HALL HOTEL
VILLAGE INN PUB
SAM'S AMERICAN DINER
BROOKES RESTAURANT
STAY AT OUR HOTEL!
Use all your powers to win a prize in Games Square!
Make sure you have an ICE day!
SNACKS
TOILETS (All include disabled)
TELEPHONE
FIRST AID
INFORMATION/ LOST CHILDREN
BUGGY/ WHEELCHAIR HIRE
CASH MACHINE
LOCKERS
RIDE PHOTOGRAPHY
PICNIC AREA
SHOP
MERLIN'S PLAYLAND
14 FALCON'S FLIGHT
Go up, up and away in your magical balloon.
15 BERTIE BASSETT'S DRIVING SCHOOL
Let your little learner drivers take the wheel of a double decker bus or fire engine and steer their way round our miniature town (extra charge).
16 JUNIOR JOUSTING HORSES
Saddle up the little ones and watch them have a galloping great time.
17 HUMAN CANNONBALL
Kids will be on this ride like a shot!
18 CLOWN AROUND
A great roundabout of fun.
19 CAROUSEL
Take the reins of a majestic stallion on this magical ride.
20 SKY DIVERS
Fly through the air with the greatest of ease.
21 KIDDIES' INDOOR PLAYLAND
Where kids can run, jump, swing & climb - the perfect place to burn off some excess energy!
22 MERLIN'S MILLIONS MAGICAL MAZE
Try to find your way to the centre of this magical attraction–then find your way out again!
23 DUNGEONS OF DOOM
A frightfully good ride in this house of horrors that could haunt you forever.
24 PICNIC PLAY AREA
Challenge someone to a giant game of draughts or Connect 4 in this fun, colourful play area.
LAND OF THE BRAVE
25 CENTURY EXCALIBUR 2
Only the most courageous should dare to ride Arthur's legendary sword, now TWICE as terrifying!
26 GAUNTLET
Will you take up the challenge to ride this fearsome looping rollercoaster?
27 DUNGEON ARCADE
Video games and slot machines.
28 THE QUINTAIN
This dastardly dizzy ride will definitely have you in a spin.
29 THE RACK
A nerve stretching experience that's pure torture, on Europe's only split roller coaster.
30 LEVERETS
A ride the little ones will love to hop on.
31 JUNIOR DRAGON COASTER
Climb on the back of this mythical creature and hold on tight!
32 JUNIOR GALLEON
Climb aboard shipmates and sail through the air!
TREATS & EATS
A EMPORIUM (King's Realm)
A treasure house of gifts, mementoes and keepsakes to remind you of your magical day.
B SMIFFY'S JOKE SHOP
(Land of the Brave) Paradise for pranksters!
C MAGIC SPELL (Knight's Valley)
A magical choice of souvenirs, from inflatable maces and toy swords to soft toys.
D FARM SHOP (Squire Bumpkin's Farm)
Cuddly toy animals and much more.
E MERLIN'S MAGICAL MIX
(Merlin's Playland)
A treat for anyone with a sweet tooth
F FACE PAINTING
(Merlin's Playland)
Guaranteed to put a smile on anyone's face.
G WALL'S ICE CREAM PARLOUR
(King's Realm) If you're partial to ice cream, this parlour's for you.
H WIMPY (King's Realm)
Enjoy great food and great value from this family favourite, inside the Castle.
I COFFEE SHOP (King's Realm)
Fresh sandwiches, hot dogs, pastries and drinks, inside the Castle.
J LANCELOT'S PLAICE
(Knight's Valley) Delicious fish & chips - the perfect place to conquer hunger.
K ICICLE WORKS
(Knight's Valley)
A mouthwatering choice of ice-creams and lollies by Wall's.
L HOT DOGS (Knight's Valley)
Tasty hot dogs.
M HOT DRINKS & SNACKS
(Knight's Valley) Tea, coffee and snacks.
N WALL'S ICES (Merlin's Playland)
Ice cream and lollies - the perfect treat.
O DRINKS & SNACKS
(Merlin's Playland)
Keep hunger at bay in Kiddies Playland.
P CASTLE HOTDOGS
(Land of the Brave)
No need to stop the fun, eat as you go.
If you want to dine in style, get a pass out from Camelot and stroll over to our Hotel.
(Check availability at Camelot's reception).
Q BROOKES RESTAURANT
(Park Hall Hotel)
Enjoy a delicious 3-course carvery lunch or dinner. Kid's menu available.
R SAM'S DINER (Park Hall Hotel)
American-themed diner for the perfect end to a perfect day. (Dinner only.)
S VILLAGE INN PUB
(Park Hall Hotel) Traditional ales and spirits. (After Park hours.)
FOOD COURT
You can pick from a feast of 5 great food choices offering great value, all in one fabulous Food Court. Located in Merlin's Playland.
WIMPY
Brilliant burgers and fantastic fries
FISH & CHIPS
The best 'chip shop' in town serving fresh battered fish and traditional pies
Have a really nice slice from our unbeatable menu of pizzas
Southern fried finger lickin' chicken pieces.
DOUWE EGBERTS
Coffee shop serving sandwiches, cakes & jacket potatoes
Visit Camelot's magical animal kingdom and get up close to lots of lovable creatures, from chipmunks and chicks to piglets and ponies.
Plus there are many interesting activities and demonstrations to enjoy:
Bottle Feeding Lambs.
Horse Grooming.
Sheep Shearing.
Hand Milking Cows and Goats.
(Feeding and demonstrations dependent on time of year.)
Squire Bumpkin's FRIENDLY FARM
VOTED LANCASHIRE FAMILY ATTRACTION OF THE YEAR 2002

Solution to key puzzle

- What differences are there between descriptions of places in stories and descriptions of places in tour guides and leaflets?

11. Now swap your leaflet with a partner. Read their tour guide carefully and write two comments. One should pick out what is particularly good about the language used or detail in the leaflet. The other should be a target to help your partner improve their tour guide.

Congratulations! You have successfully completed your whistle-stop tour of detailed descriptions, impressive information texts and excellent explanations. You have also used your writing skills to produce your very own tour guide.

UNIT 5

Campaign capers

This unit asks you to take up the campaign challenge and show off your persuasive writing skills. After investigating a variety of leaflets and adverts, you are invited to take the plunge and devise your very own campaign to publicise a cartoon-based computer game for the 21st century.

5.1 Catching the reader's interest

Key puzzle

- How do writers attempt to persuade the reader when presenting adverts on paper?

Remember!

- **Persuasion** is when you present something in order to get people to act in a certain way.
- **Comparing** is where we identify the similarities between two texts.
- **Contrasting** is where we identify the differences between two texts.

An advertiser's dream

1. Think about some advertisements you have seen in newspapers, magazines or on billboards recently. What kind of information would you expect to see on these kinds of adverts?

2. Feed back your ideas to the class and keep a class list of features for later reference.

Catching the eye of the reader

3. Look at the two adverts below. Both are trying to persuade us to do something in a particular way. What is each advert trying to advertise?

4. Look at the Oxy advert. What impact does the title have on you?
5. Now look at the Barnado's advert. What impact does the picture have on you?

5.1

6. Using a grid like the one below, note down what the two adverts have in common – the similarities – and where they differ.

Similarities	Differences

7. What kind of 'audience' do you think each advert is aimed at?
8. Look closely at the language used in both. Which words are used to really persuade the reader? Make a list of these for use when you create your own persuasive pieces.
9. If you could alter the Oxy advert, what would you add or change? Why?

Solution to key puzzle

- How do writers attempt to persuade the reader when presenting adverts on paper?

10. With a partner, make a list of all the persuasive techniques you have spotted in these adverts. Think about:
    - layout
    - language
    - images
    - font size.
11. Share your ideas with another pair, and devise five top tips for a new advertisement designer.

5.2 Campaign tips

Key puzzle

- How do writers make an impact on their readers when presenting information on an issue or a new product?

Remember!

- **Explanation** is explaining how or why something happens.
- A **campaign** is a series of activities designed to achieve a particular outcome.

We have impact!

1. A campaign has to grab the interest of its target audience. Look at the web page below. What kind of audience do you think this is appealing to?

TUSSAUD'S CHESSINGTON WORLD of ADVENTURES

INFO

BOOKING

EXPLORE

FUNSTUFF

New FOR 2002

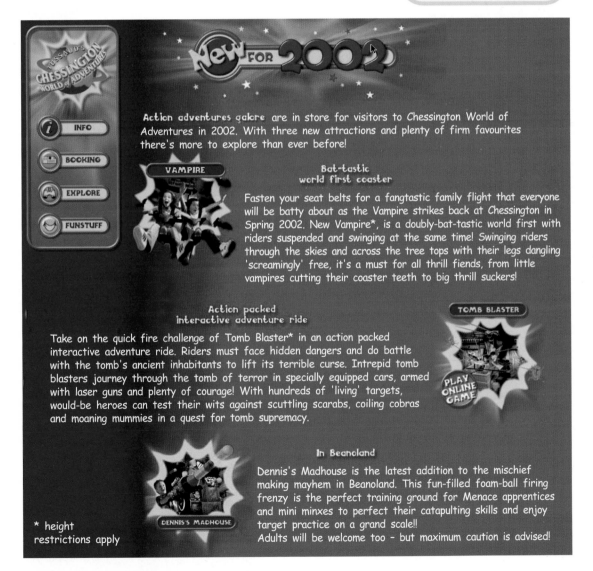

Action adventures galore are in store for visitors to Chessington World of Adventures in 2002. With three new attractions and plenty of firm favourites there's more to explore than ever before!

VAMPIRE

Bat-tastic
world first coaster

Fasten your seat belts for a fangtastic family flight that everyone will be batty about as the Vampire strikes back at Chessington in Spring 2002. New Vampire*, is a doubly-bat-tastic world first with riders suspended and swinging at the same time! Swinging riders through the skies and across the tree tops with their legs dangling 'screamingly' free, it's a must for all thrill fiends, from little vampires cutting their coaster teeth to big thrill suckers!

Action packed
interactive adventure ride

Take on the quick fire challenge of Tomb Blaster* in an action packed interactive adventure ride. Riders must face hidden dangers and do battle with the tomb's ancient inhabitants to lift its terrible curse. Intrepid tomb blasters journey through the tomb of terror in specially equipped cars, armed with laser guns and plenty of courage! With hundreds of 'living' targets, would-be heroes can test their wits against scuttling scarabs, coiling cobras and moaning mummies in a quest for tomb supremacy.

TOMB BLASTER

PLAY ONLINE GAME

In Beanoland

Dennis's Madhouse is the latest addition to the mischief making mayhem in Beanoland. This fun-filled foam-ball firing frenzy is the perfect training ground for Menace apprentices and mini minxes to perfect their catapulting skills and enjoy target practice on a grand scale!!
Adults will be welcome too – but maximum caution is advised!

DENNIS'S MADHOUSE

* height restrictions apply

2. Imagine you are a marketing director at a theme park. You are in charge of a campaign to advertise new features. What other methods might you use to advertise them?

Planning the campaign

3. Read the article below, taken from the RSPCA's website. It explains a number of ideas and tips about running a successful campaign based on a good cause or an issue.

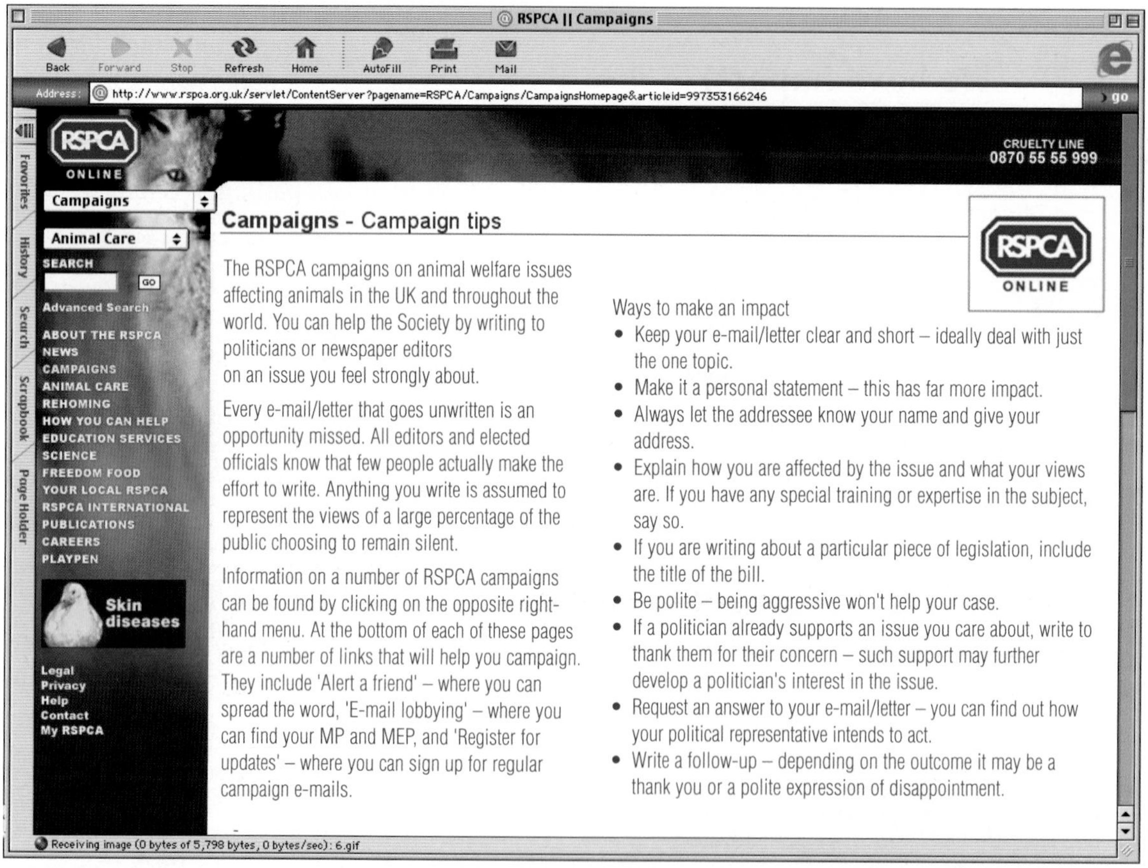

RSPCA || Campaigns

Back Forward Stop Refresh Home AutoFill Print Mail

Address: http://www.rspca.org.uk/servlet/ContentServer?pagename=RSPCA/Campaigns/CampaignsHomepage&articleid=997353166246

RSPCA ONLINE

CRUELTY LINE 0870 55 55 999

Campaigns

Animal Care

SEARCH

Advanced Search

ABOUT THE RSPCA
NEWS
CAMPAIGNS
ANIMAL CARE
REHOMING
HOW YOU CAN HELP
EDUCATION SERVICES
SCIENCE
FREEDOM FOOD
YOUR LOCAL RSPCA
RSPCA INTERNATIONAL
PUBLICATIONS
CAREERS
PLAYPEN

Skin diseases

Legal
Privacy
Help
Contact
My RSPCA

Campaigns - Campaign tips

The RSPCA campaigns on animal welfare issues affecting animals in the UK and throughout the world. You can help the Society by writing to politicians or newspaper editors on an issue you feel strongly about.

Every e-mail/letter that goes unwritten is an opportunity missed. All editors and elected officials know that few people actually make the effort to write. Anything you write is assumed to represent the views of a large percentage of the public choosing to remain silent.

Information on a number of RSPCA campaigns can be found by clicking on the opposite right-hand menu. At the bottom of each of these pages are a number of links that will help you campaign. They include 'Alert a friend' – where you can spread the word, 'E-mail lobbying' – where you can find your MP and MEP, and 'Register for updates' – where you can sign up for regular campaign e-mails.

Ways to make an impact

- Keep your e-mail/letter clear and short – ideally deal with just the one topic.
- Make it a personal statement – this has far more impact.
- Always let the addressee know your name and give your address.
- Explain how you are affected by the issue and what your views are. If you have any special training or expertise in the subject, say so.
- If you are writing about a particular piece of legislation, include the title of the bill.
- Be polite – being aggressive won't help your case.
- If a politician already supports an issue you care about, write to thank them for their concern – such support may further develop a politician's interest in the issue.
- Request an answer to your e-mail/letter – you can find out how your political representative intends to act.
- Write a follow-up – depending on the outcome it may be a thank you or a polite expression of disappointment.

Receiving image (0 bytes of 5,798 bytes, 0 bytes/sec): 6.gif

4. Study the list of suggested ways of making an impact.
   - Which of these could you use as part of an advertising campaign?
   - Which would *not* be appropriate as part of an advertising campaign?

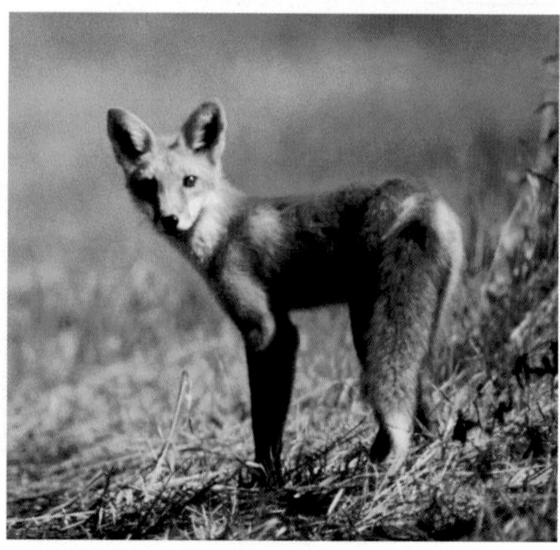

5.2

5. Now look back at the theme park advert on page 85. Thinking about campaigning for a cause and for a new product, devise two separate lists suggesting the aspects you would include in your campaigns. Use grids like the ones below.

The campaign for a good cause

Possible elements of campaign (What?)	Where?	Audience?	How will I know if it's successful?

The campaign to help sell a new product

Possible elements of campaign (What?)	Where?	Audience?	How will I know if it's successful?
(bullet points)			

Solution to key puzzle

- How do writers make an impact on their readers when presenting information on an issue or a new product?

6. With a partner, summarise these points and devise your own 'Ways to Make an Impact' checklist of essential elements to include in a campaign.

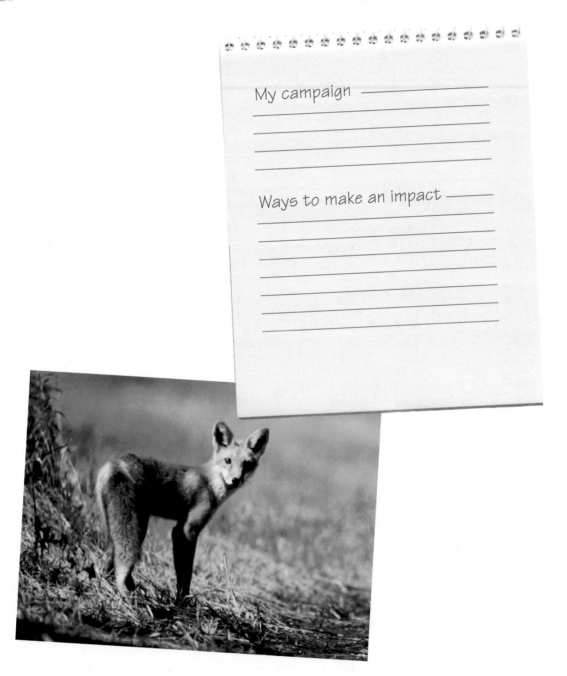

My campaign

Ways to make an impact

5.3 The campaign challenge!

Key puzzle – part 1

- What skills are needed to plan a campaign for a new cartoon-based computer game?

Remember!

- **Collating** is where we bring ideas from different sources together.
- **Classifying** is where we group information together in categories.
- **Planning** is where we prepare our writing with lists, brainstorms, etc.

Catch up on classic characters

1. Look at the classic characters below. With a partner, take turns to tell each other what you know about these characters and their adventures, spending no more than 30 seconds on each one.

2. Make a list of characters and include the most important piece of information about each one.
3. Now classify the characters by sorting them into groups, e.g. villains, heroes, people.
4. Feed back your groupings to the rest of the class. Which group has the most characters? Why do you think this group is more popular?

Planning the campaign

5.3

5. Now choose one of these characters and fill in a character information grid like the one below.

Picture of character and name	Information on character and adventures

5.3

6. Now think about how you might change the characteristics and adventures of one of these characters to make them more appealing to a modern audience. Make a note of your ideas in a grid like the one below.

Character	New characteristics	New ideas for adventures

7. Using the example below, think about how you might build the character into a new computer game.

5.4

8. Plan your ideas, using the model below to help you.

Name of computer game	
Aims of game	
Role of cartoon character	
Special features of game	
Target audience	

Solution to key puzzle

- What skills are needed to plan a campaign for a new cartoon-based computer game?

9. With a partner, think about all the skills you have used to plan out the ideas for your computer game. Jot down a list of these.

10. Now think about the actual campaign designed to persuade people to buy the computer game. What skills do you predict you will need to use to plan your publicity road-show?

5.4 On the campaign trail

Key puzzle – part 2

- What skills are needed to plan a campaign for a new cartoon-based computer game?

Remember!

- **Planning** is where we prepare our writing with lists, brainstorms, etc.
- **Persuasion** is when you present something in order to get people to act in a certain way.
- A **campaign** is a series of activities designed to achieve a particular outcome.
- **Structure** is the framework we give a piece of writing which gives it 'shape' and makes it easier to follow.

New tricks for a new audience

1. Think about something you have considered buying recently. Have you seen or heard it advertised anywhere, e.g. on TV, on a poster, on other products, such as the back of a crisp packet?

   Note down where you saw the advertising and which type you think has most impact on you.
2. What kinds of special offers most often convince us to buy?
3. Which of these types of advertising and offers would have the most impact on you?

4. Feed back your ideas and create a class reference list of types of advertising, and offers that interest your age group.

Perfect persuasion

You already have ideas for your game. Now you need to plan your advertising campaign.

5.5 **5.** Note down the different elements (types of advertising) of your campaign. You must have more than one.

Type of advertising	*Where people will see advert*	*Audience this will appeal to*

6. Now take one type of advertisement, e.g. a flyer, poster, TV advert, radio advert, website info. Plan the layout and/or text for this. Look at the model below to give you some ideas.

5.6 **7.** Now, using the structure below, explain how you will organise your campaign and what persuasive techniques you will use to promote your game.

The new computer game I want to promote is called ____________________________ .

The game is aimed at ____ .

The main features of the game are ____ .

My campaign to promote this product will consist of ________________ sections.

First, I will have ____ .

Then, I will ____ .

Finally, I will ____ .

Solution to key puzzle

- What skills are needed to plan a campaign for a new cartoon-based computer game?

8. Now, in small groups, present your ideas. Make sure you explain your designs and campaign plans clearly and with enthusiasm.

5.7 **9.** Give each group a mark out of ten for ideas and for presentation skills.

10. When each group has presented, collect your marks and write yourself a target for presenting in the future.

11. Feed back to the rest of the class on whose presentation was best and why.

Congratulations! You have successfully completed the campaign challenge and practised your persuasive writing skills to perfection!

Can you judge a book by its cover?

This unit introduces you to a range of narrative extracts and how writers create different effects for different styles of writing. Once you have navigated your way through styles like horror, war and mystery writing, you can pick up your pen and practise the different styles in your own writing.

Cover stories

Key puzzle

- How do readers 'identify' the type of story they are reading?

Remember!

- **Text** means the words that are used.
- An **image** is a picture or part of a picture.
- **Layout** is the arrangement of text and pictures on a page.
- **Prediction** is when we make guesses based on evidence.

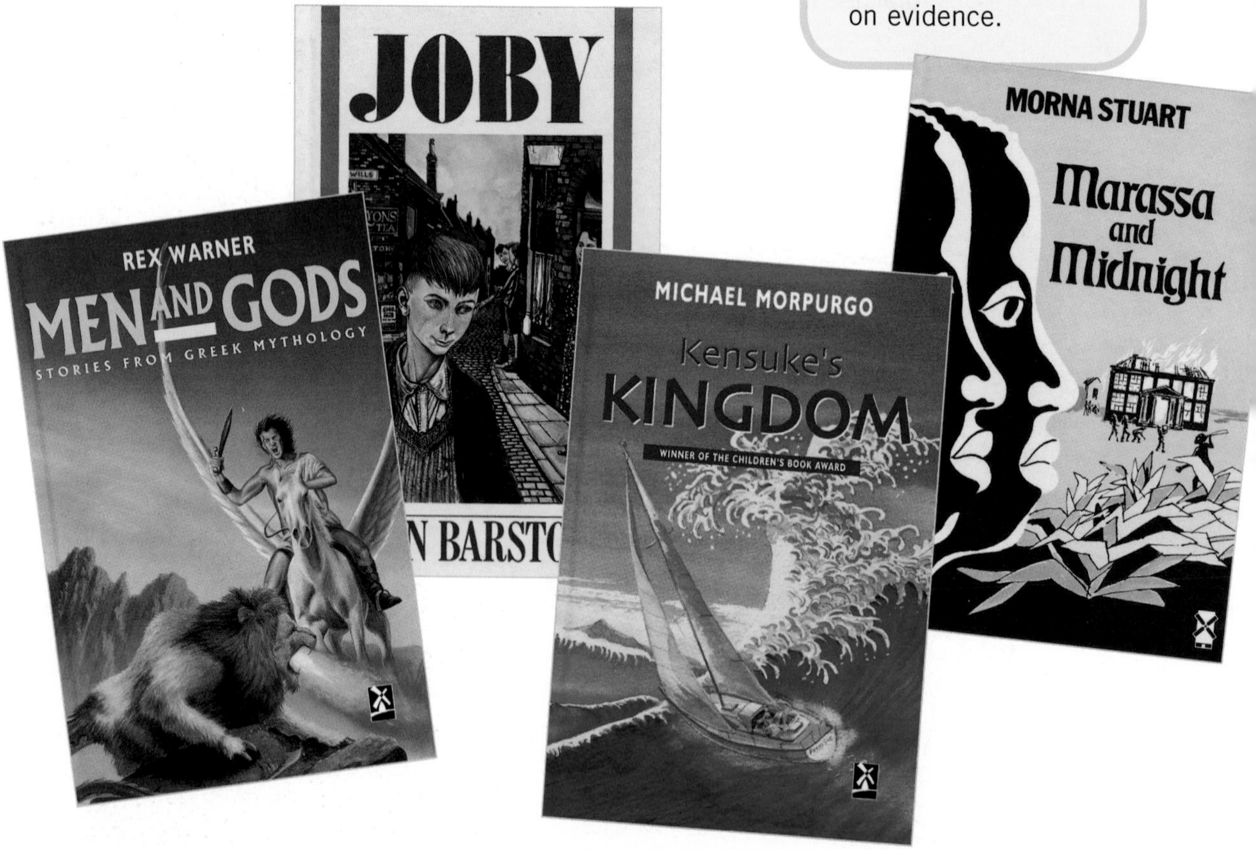

Reading the pictures

1. With a partner, look at the book covers below.

   What kind of book do you think each is? Crime? Horror?

   What clues in the titles/pictures make you think this?

2. Feed back your ideas to the rest of the class. Are there any covers that don't make it clear what the book is, or where it could be any one of a variety of types?
3. Choose one of the covers. Predict what the storyline might be and how it might end. Jot down your notes to refer back to later.

It's all a blurb

We have already discovered we can make predictions based on our observations of front covers. We can also learn a lot about a book from the blurb on the back cover.

4. With a partner, look at the back covers printed below. Jot down notes on what you notice about these.

6.1

You should think about:

- the size of the print
- the amount of text
- reviews or comments from other writers or reviewers
- sections of the text that have been reprinted
- questions left unanswered.

EMPIRE OF THE SUN

Empire of the Sun is a gripping, hallucinatory vision of war. Through the eyes of a ten-year-old boy stranded in Shanghai J.G. Ballard portrays the chaos and confusion of a world torn apart.
"I have never read a novel which gave me a stronger sense of the helplessness of war. It is haunting in its pictures and its atmosphere is unforgettable" Observer
"The best British novel about the Second World War" Guardian

MY FRIEND WALTER

When a mysterious invitation lands on the doorstep, Bess goes to a family reunion in London. Bess's visit to the Tower of London is just the start of a series of unusual events. Who is the stranger in the black cloak who is so keen to talk to her? Can Bess keep her friendly ghost a secret from her family? And does he have anything to do with the theft of the crown jewels?

RED SKY IN THE MORNING

As long as I live, I shall never forget the night my brother was born

When Anna's brother Ben is born disabled her family's joy at the birth is touched with sadness. Although Anna loves Ben she is afraid of what her friends will say at school and tries to hide him from the outside world. But it is Ben's bubbly love of life which gives her the strength not only to face up to his disability but to deal with her own teenage concerns at home and school.

Fifty-Fifty Tutti-Frutti Chocolate-Chip

This collection of engaging short stories reflects a broad range of cultures, diverse topics and literary styles.
Especially selected to appeal to Key Stage 3 students, the collection includes:

- humorous stories
- chilling urban myths
- tales with a twist
- stories from different genres

Stimulating activities enable students to explore the stories and encourage comparisons between them. The wide range of established authors includes Norman Silver, Farrukh Dhondy and Brian Friel.

"This outstanding collection reinforces my belief that people in different cultures are none other than ourselves with different accents and in different clothes and situations."
Norman Silver

You might like to record your ideas in a grid like the one below.

	Book 1	Book 2	Book 3	Book 4
The size of print or amount of text				
Reviews or comments from other writers or reviewers				
Sections of the text that have been reprinted				
Questions left unanswered				
Other comments				

5. Share your ideas with the rest of the class.

6. How many different ways can you think of to finish the following statement:
6.1 *Book covers help a reader to find out more about a book by …*

7. As a class, decide on the best statements and display them in your classroom.

6.2 **8.** Now, thinking about a book you have read, and using a book jacket frame like the one below, design a front cover and blurb that give clues to your readers about what kind of book it is. (You don't have to draw the cover, you can describe what the pictures would be.)

Solution to key puzzle

- How do readers 'identify' the type of story they are reading?

9. Now swap your book cover with a partner. Take it in turns to guess what the book is about and the kind of story/characters that might develop. Explain what clues are making you think this.

10. Give marks out of ten for good predictions. Which things helped the reader make their guesses?

6.2 Stylish writing

Key puzzle

- What clues do writers leave to help the reader guess what kind of story they are reading?

Remember!

- **Genre** is the word we use to define a type or style of writing, e.g. horror.
- **Tone** is the word we use to explain the 'sound' of a piece of writing, e.g. scary, funny, sad.

Great expectations!

6.3

1. Look at the list of different story genres below. Choose a couple from this list and brainstorm what you would expect to find in this kind of text, i.e. what kind of characters, what kind of story line, what kind of setting?

crime

fantasy

mystery

romance

fable

adventure

2. Share your brainstorm notes with the rest of the class. Are there any differences of opinion about these expectations?

Guess the genre

Often when we read stories, we can guess what kind of tale they are going to be. We know this from the kinds of characters we are introduced to, or the kind of language used. For example, if a story starts 'Once upon a time', we know automatically that we are about to read a fairy tale.

3. Read this extract from the opening of a science fiction story; then read the notes around it.

Opens with panicky speech to throw reader straight into tense situation.

Use of exclamation marks to signify tension in passage.

Use of word 'vessels' creates sense of mystery. What type of vessels?

> 'Quick, quick! The engine's on fire and we have unfriendly vessels making ground on us! It's only a matter of time before they launch an attack. Permission to open fire, sir. We cannot afford to wait!'
> The Captain took a moment before replying to his flight lieutenant. 'Permission denied, Zorb. We will not break the Federation code!'

The words 'permission to open fire, sir' establish a war-type situation and rank of different characters.

The name 'Zorb' suggests an alien character.

Use of word 'Federation' links with ruling bodies in space travel stories.

6.4

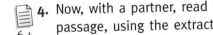

4. Now, with a partner, read the passage below from a school story. Make notes on the passage, using the extract above as a model.

> 'Wicked! Wait till I tell H. He'll be dead jealous!' Marty smirked and sniffed as if he'd just stepped in something unpleasant. 'Yeah, well – there's a bonus then for the little creep.' I shifted uncomfortably and plunged my hands deeper into my pockets. H was my best mate, but I knew Marty hated him and took every opportunity to let him know. I didn't want to become involved in their feud, but neither could I let this chance of a lifetime pass me by.

Top tip: A really good way to help establish what genre a piece of narrative belongs to, is to think about what kinds of films and TV programmes use the same images and language.

5. With a partner, read the extracts below. As you read, think about the characters and settings created and the language used.

Extract 1

He used poisons, and some of the worst magic he'd learned, and he made this thing that he called a dog – it looked something like a dog. But it was so black that you couldn't really see it, and its eyes shone all the time like a real dog's eyes do when light catches them – shone red, or green, and sometimes blue. It was big.

From *Feeding The Dog* by Susan Price

Extract 2

He saw the helicopters in his rear-view mirror; they darted like vultures waiting for a death to feed upon. His heart ran riot and he looked in the mirror again; he could see the helicopters drawing closer. The nearer they drew, the more certain his death became. Then all about him were flames.

From *Soldier* by Ben Rayner

Extract 3

But now, a year later, the urge to look back was too great.

Only a snatched, split-second look as he turned his head. But what he saw was burned in his mind for the instant he had left to live. To his right he looked, straight into burning eyes set in a skull behind a helmet resting, weighing down on his shoulder. And he felt the grip of bony hands inside the gauntlets grip harder into his waist and an inexorable pull from behind. And he seemed to see a huddled bundle rise from the road behind him and a standing figure smiling with satisfaction.

From *Crossing* by Dennis Hamley

Extract 4

And then she was running after him towards the lake, passing him and getting ahead since he was already winded, and he was fifty yards behind her when she reached the edge, ran into the water and swam strongly towards the spot where for a moment the back of the boy's head showed at the surface.

She was there in a few strokes and had him and then, as she put her feet down to tread water for the turn, he saw with sudden sheer horror – a horror mirrored in his wife's blue eyes – that she was standing on the bottom, holding their dead son, in only three feet of water.

From *Nightmare in Blue* by Fredric Brown

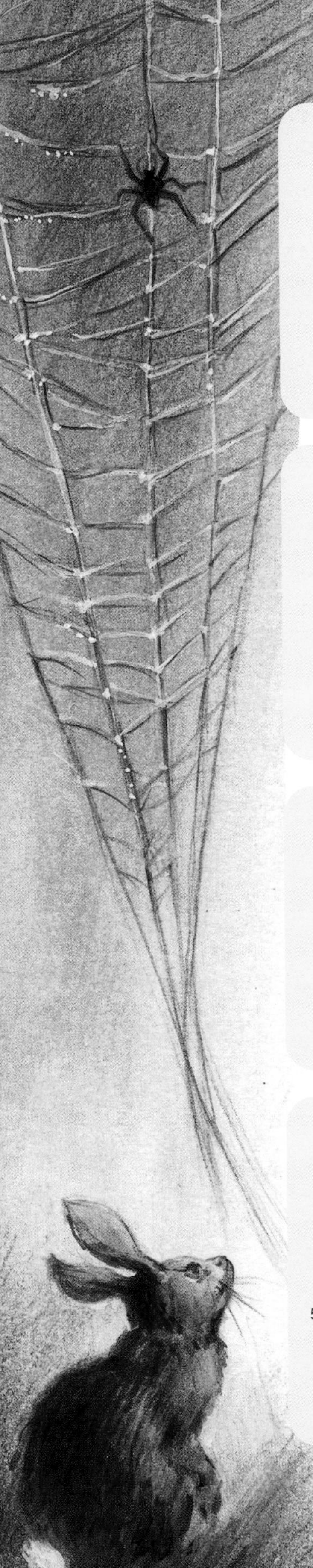

Extract 5

The edge of the swamp was a mass of bodies. The rising moon shone on their leather hides and was reflected in their eyes. Colin could see white shapes spreading out on either side to encircle the rock; they were in no hurry now, for they knew that escape was impossible.

From *The Weirdstone of Brisingamen* by Alan Garner

Extract 6

So Spider began to spin, and very soon he was lost to sight high above them all with only the ladder of silver thread to show them the way he had gone. Presently Hare declared that all was ready and, leading the way, he began to climb up into the sky followed by all the other animals.

From *Spider's Web* by Kathleen Arnott

Extract 7

It had stopped snowing. John stood at the door, watching the stranger until he was out of sight. Then, as he turned to go indoors, he was filled with wonder; for he saw that where the stranger had walked, there were no footprints in the snow.

From *The Christmas Gift* by Hugh Oliver

Extract 8

The magician and his brother rode through the mists toward the secret place.

'We shouldn't have come,' Caramon muttered. His large, strong hand was on the hilt of his great sword, and his eyes searched every shadow. 'I have been in many dangerous places, but nothing to equal this!'

From *The Test of the Twins* by Margaret Weis

6. Now you have read all the extracts, see if you can guess what story 'genre' each one comes from. You might want to suggest more than one genre if you can't make a final decision.

6.5 7. What clues in the text helped you decide on the genre? Fill in a grid like the one below, explaining your decisions.

	Genre	Clues
Extract 1	*Fantasy or Horror*	*He used poisons, and some of the worst magic he'd learned, and he made this thing that he called a dog*
Extract 2		
Extract 3		
Extract 4		
Extract 5		
Extract 6		
Extract 7		
Extract 8		

8. Feedback your ideas to the class. Which extracts were difficult to guess? Why?

As well as the *ideas in stories*, the *words writers use* and *the way they say things* help us guess what kind of story it is going to be.

9. Read the extract below.

> The front door swung open. A blast of cold wind swept in over me. So cold, I thought. From now on, will I feel only cold? Will I never feel warm again? My whole body shivered. I turned and saw Jake shivering too. His eyes were shut, his teeth chattering.

10. What do you notice about the sentences the author uses?

11. Which particular words do you think the writer wants us to focus on?

12. What kind of mood (atmosphere) is being built up here?

13. As a class, create the next sentence. Try to keep the same tone to the piece.

14. With a partner, write the next two sentences.

15. Share your sentences with the class. Which sentences fit best? Why?

16. Now look at the sentences the author chose to use:

> Someone pushed me hard, away from the doorway. The ghouls were limping, staggering, groaning, making their way out of the house.

Was this what you expected? Does this give the reader any more clues about the type of story it is?

Solution to key puzzle

- What clues do writers leave to help the reader guess what kind of story they are reading?

17. Now, with a partner, look at all the clues listed below that might help us guess what kind of story we are reading.

> **Clues:** book cover, title, blurb, character names, place names, character descriptions, setting descriptions, types of sentences throughout, first sentence, last sentence, tone.

6.6 Discuss these clues and then place them on the 'story hints' thermometer, showing which ideas are most useful in leaving 'genre clues' for the reader.
The best clues should go at the top of the thermometer.

18. Feed back your ideas to the rest of the class. Which elements do you think are the best clues to help you guess the genre?

6.3 Write on!

Key puzzle

- What do writers need to remember to create the right tone in their writing?

Remember!

- **Genre** is the word we use to define a type or style of writing.
- **Structure** is the word we use to explain how we organise a piece of writing.
- **Image** is the word we use to describe the picture that is painted with words.

How many ways can you say ...?

1. Read the paragraph below. With a partner, see how many ways you can rewrite it to create different effects.

6.7

You can change words, word order and leave some parts out if you wish to change the tone of the piece.

> The man rose from his seat. He looked around with his flashing green eyes. He raised the hand that was holding the 'thing'. The dark cave was eerie. The girls looked around for the boys to help them. A sound came from nowhere. It was quite frightening.

2. Share your ideas with the rest of the class. What effects have been created by changing some of the words and the word order?

Creating the right image

3. Now read the short passage below. Which words create the sounds and images of war? Which words and phrases create the best image for the reader?

> Anti-aircraft guns barked on and on, like a pack of cheated hounds. There were more of them than there used to be, but they weren't making much difference. Chas watched fragments of cork dropping off the shelter wall. He counted them as they lay on the floor. Anything to keep his mind off things.
>
> From *The Machine Gunners* by Robert Westall

Descriptions of images and sounds play an important part in creating the image of a setting. Other senses are important, too.

6.8

4. Choose a genre: horror, ghost, adventure, romance, fairy tale, mystery, crime, fantasy.

   Now, using a grid like the one on the next page, plan the words, phrases and ideas you would use to describe a main *setting* in your story.

   The grid has been divided into three sections so that you can think of words that describe:

   - the overview (like a camera's long shot)
   - the specific detail of a place (like a medium camera shot)
   - the very fine detail of objects or places (like a close-up shot).

	Thoughts and emotions	What you can see	What you can hear	What you can feel/ touch	What you can smell
Overview (long shot)					
Specific detail (mid shot)					
Fine detail (close up)					

6.8

5. Now write up your setting description. Think about what you have learned about how writers leave clues about the genre of their writing. Try to create the right image for your chosen genre.

   Remember, you are just trying to create the setting description, not write the story.

Solution to key puzzle

- What do writers need to remember to create the right tone in their writing?

6. When you have finished your descriptive piece, swap work with a partner. Comment on how well they have described their setting and established their chosen genre.
7. Write three targets for your partner, suggesting ways they might improve their work and establish their genre more clearly.

Congratulations! You have examined how writers use language to create different effects for different styles of writing. You have also experimented with this in your own writing.

You are now on your way to being a cracking good writer!

Snappy spelling challenges

This section challenges you to learn, improve and test your spelling by revising key spelling rules and practising spelling patterns. If you work your way through the challenges, you'll be on your way to being a super speller!

Challenge 1: *plural power*

Remember!

- A **noun** is the name of a person, object or feeling.
- **Singular** means only one.
- **Plural** means more than one.
- **Vowels** are a e i o u (sometimes y).
- **Consonants** are letters other than vowels.

Plurals 1

Generally, when we want to make a noun plural, we add **-s**.

Plurals with an -s		Other types of plurals	
book	book**s**	box	box**es**
ruler	ruler**s**	bus	bus**es**
desk	desk**s**	church	church**es**
coat	coat**s**	dish	dish**es**
pen	pen**s**		
card	card**s**		
school	school**s**		
sister	sister**s**		
brother	brother**s**		

Sometimes, we add **-es**. This is when there is a hissing or buzzing sound at the end of the word or when we need to add another syllable, e.g. bus**es**.

Challenge

C1

Sort the nouns below into those that need **-s** and those that need **-es** to make them plural.

- boy
- witch
- patch
- glass
- kiss
- watch
- girl
- fox
- class
- lunch
- lamp
- table

Plurals 2

If a word ends in **-f** or **-fe** we usually do something different.

-f and -fe endings	
half	halves
life	lives
scarf	scarves

As you can see, we remove the **-f/-fe** and add **-ves**.

Challenge

Can you change the following into plurals?

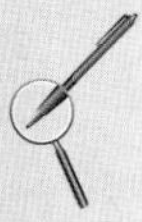

C1

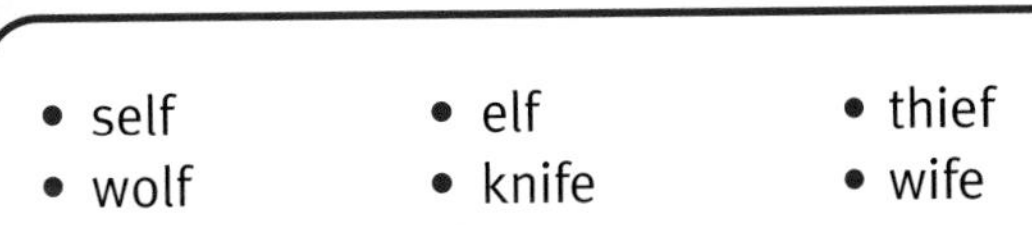

- self
- wolf
- elf
- knife
- thief
- wife

Plurals 3

If words end in **-y** we have to look very carefully.
If there is a vowel before the **-y**, then we just add **-s**.
If there is a consonant before the **-y**, we remove the **-y** and add **-ies**.

Vowel + **-y** words		Consonant + **-y** words	
boy	boys	baby	babies
toy	toys	city	cities
day	days	lorry	lorries
key	keys	party	parties
monkey	monkeys		
tray	trays		

Challenge

C1

How many other words can you think of to go in both columns?
Write both the singular and the plural.

Challenge 2: *doubling is troubling*

Remember!

- **Vowels** are a e i o u (sometimes y).
- **Consonants** are letters other than vowels.
- A **syllable** is each beat in a word.
- A **base word** is a word we can build on to create new words.
- **Long vowels** are the *names* of the letters a e i o u.
- **Short vowels** are the *sounds* of the letters a e i o u, e.g. 'o' as in 'top'.

Doubling 1

When we want to build on a word with an **-ed, -est**, **-er** or **-ing** ending, we have to be careful. Sometimes we double the last letter of the base word and sometimes we don't.

Generally, the rule to remember is:

When the word has a short vowel and ends in a single consonant, we double the last letter before adding new endings:

e.g. dig   di**gg**ing.

But when the word has a long vowel before the last consonant, we do not double the last letter before adding new endings:

e.g. feel   fee**l**ing.

Challenge

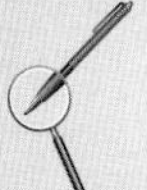

C2

Place the following words in a grid like the one below. For each word, show whether you have doubled the last letter before placing it in the grid (write the original word and then the adapted word).

You only need to put a word in one of the columns, even if it fits in more than one.

- beg
- drain
- drag
- train
- top
- wet
- beep
- shop
- plan
- big
- drop
- skip
- hum
- fit

-ed	-er	-est	-ing
			weep – weeping

Challenge

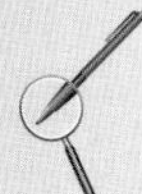

C2

Can you come up with your own list of words to be placed in the grid? Challenge your partner to place them correctly.

Challenge 3: *proper endings*

Remember!

- **Vowels** are a e i o u (sometimes y).
- **Consonants** are letters other than vowels.
- A **base word** is a word we can build on to create new words.
- A **suffix** is an ending that changes the base word.

Suffixes 1

Often we want to add to a base word to make other words, using groups of letters such as **-al**, **-ary**, **-ic**, **-ist**, **-ive**, **-est**. These are called **vowel suffixes**, as they are added on to the end of a word and they start with a vowel.

If the base word ends in a consonant, we just add the vowel suffix:

e.g. season season**al**.

If the base word ends in the vowel **-e**, we remove this before adding the vowel suffix:

e.g. expense expens**ive**.

If the base word ends in the letter **-y**, we change this to **-i** before adding the vowel suffix:

e.g. funny funni**est**.

Challenge

See if you can add a vowel suffix to the following words:

- acid
- diction
- person
- balloon
- addition
- nation
- detect
- machine
- medic
- happy
- occasion
- exception

Suffixes 2

With some words we add the suffixes **-ible** and **-able** to create a new word. The best way to remember which one to use is to ask 'Are you able to do it?' If the answer is 'Yes' then generally you add **-able**, e.g. enjoy becomes enjoyable. Words that don't follow this rule tend to end in **-ible**, e.g. terror becomes terri**ble**.

Challenge

C3

Can you devise a list of words that use **-able** and words that take **-ible** to make new words?

Suffixes 3

We can also add to base words using **consonant suffixes**. These are added on to the end of the word and begin with a consonant:

e.g. **-ly**, **-ful**, **-less**, **-ness**.

Most words stay the same when we add **-ly**, **-ful** and **-less**:

e.g.		
	actual	actual**ly**
	meaning	meaning**ful**
	hope	hope**less**

Sometimes if a word ends in a consonant plus **-y**, we change the **-y** to **-i** and then add the suffix:

e.g. happy   happiness.

Challenge

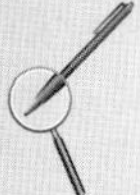

C3

Can you add one of the consonant suffixes to the following words (some may work with more than one suffix)?

- beauty
- harm
- friend
- home
- care
- eventual
- hope
- week
- forget
- hateful
- head
- play
- fear
- thank
- care
- colour
- kind

Challenge 4: *good beginnings*

Remember!

- **Vowels** are a e i o u (sometimes y).
- **Consonants** are letters other than vowels.
- A **base word** is a word we can build on to create new words.
- A **prefix** is an addition to the beginning of a word, which changes the base word.
- An **antonym** is a word that has the opposite meaning to another word.

Prefixes 1

Often we want to add to the beginning of a base word to make other words, using particular groups of letters, e.g. **in-**, **im-**, **ir-**, **il-**, **mis-**, **non-**, **un-**, **anti-**. These are called **antonym prefixes**, as they are added on to the beginning of a word and give it the opposite meaning.

When we add an antonym prefix, we do not change the spelling of the base word. Therefore a word beginning with **n** and added to with **un** will have two **n**s, e.g. **unn**atural, and a word beginning with **s** and added to with **mis** will have two **s**s, e.g. **miss**pelt.

Challenge

Can you add an antonym prefix to the following words?

- regular
- helpful
- reasonable
- legal
- freeze
- possible
- place
- mature
- tidy

Prefixes 2

Some prefixes have particular meanings that give us a clue about the meaning of a word:

e.g. bi = two, so bicycle = two wheels.

Challenge

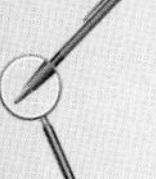

C4

Look at the table below and see if you can find words to attach the particular prefixes below to.

Prefixes	Meanings
anti	against
bi	two
pre	before
de	undo
inter	between
sub	under
mis	wrong
re	again
ex	out of

Challenge 5: *sounds like ...*

Remember!

- A **homophone** is a word that sounds the same as another but is spelt differently and has a different meaning.
- A **strategy** is a trick or a method of doing something.
- A **definition** is the meaning of a word.

Homophones 1

These words are important to learn, as knowing which one to use can really improve your work.

Challenge

C5

Look at the list below. Make sure you know what each word means, then try to find a strategy to help you remember them. (There is some advice on different strategies on pages 125 and 126.)

• by	• buy	• bye
• their	• they're	• there
• rein	• rain	• reign
• too	• two	• to
• your	• you're	• yore

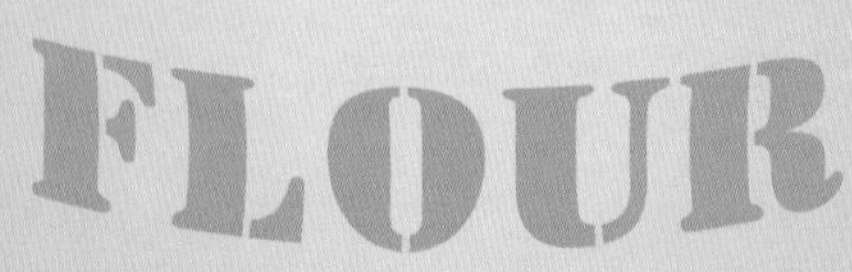

Challenge

Below are some other words that are homophones. Can you find the homophone to match each word in the table? Jot down what each word means.

Word	Meaning	Word	Meaning
aloud	not silent	allowed	permitted
are		our	
board			
		brake	
		blew	
hole			
hour			
		not	
know			
		maid	
flour			
		great	
hair			
		heard	
new			
		meat	
peace			
		threw	
right			
		tale	
pane			
here			

Challenge 6: *something missing?*

Remember!

- An **apostrophe** is a punctuation mark used to show omission or possession.
- **Omission** means that something has been left out.
- **Possession** means 'belonging to'. We use an apostrophe and an **s** (**'s**) to show that something belongs to someone.

When we speak we often shorten words or join words together, e.g. **do not** becomes **don't**.

When we write the shortened word, we must *insert an apostrophe at the exact place where the letter or letters have been missed out*, e.g. **cannot** becomes **can't**.

Challenge

C6

Look at the words below. Write the shortened word beside each one, with the apostrophe in the right place.

I am
you are
he is
they are
I have
could not
does not
had not
have not
it is

Challenge 7: *that belongs to someone!*

Remember!

- An **apostrophe** is a punctuation mark used to show omission or possession.
- **Omission** means that something has been left out.
- **Possession** means 'belonging to'. We use an apostrophe and an **s** (**'s**) to show that something belongs to someone.

If we want to show that one person or thing owns something we add an apostrophe + s ('s), e.g. the man's case = the case belonging to the man.

If we want to show more than one person or thing owns something:

1. First, we make the word plural:

the boy	the boy**s**
the lady	the lad**ies**
the bus	the bus**es**
the child	the child**ren**
the mouse	the **mice**

2. Then, if the plural word ends in -s, just put an apostrophe after it:

the boy	the boy**s**	the boy**s'** school
the lady	the lad**ies**	the lad**ies'** clothes
the bus	the bus**es**	the bus**es'** tyres

3. If the plural doesn't end in -s, we add apostrophe and s:

the child	the child**ren**	the child**ren's** toys
the mouse	the **mice**	the **mice's** tails

Challenge

See if you can place an apostrophe in the right place in the list below. Be warned – some might have more than one answer. If they do, explain why.

the mans coat
the dogs bone
the womans house
the cars wheel
the rooms doors
the peoples thoughts
the shops windows
the books pages
the trees leaves
the cats basket

Spelling Hot Spot Warning! If we write about something belonging to it, e.g. its door, its page, we do *not* add an apostrophe as the word would look the same as the abbreviated **it is** – **it's**.

Challenge 8: *memory tricks*

Remember!

- A **strategy** is a trick or a method of doing something.
- A **definition** is the meaning of a word.

Memory tricks 1

Most people find different ways of remembering spellings.
Sometimes they remember the rule, sometimes they look at the different parts of a word, e.g. the prefix and the suffix, but at other times they can use different 'memory tricks'. These are called **mnemonics**. They are memory strategies to help you remember the sequence of letters in a word, e.g:

- **because** = **b**ig **e**lephants **c**an't **a**lways **u**se **s**mall **e**xits.
- **necessary** = **n**ever **e**at **c**hips, **e**at **s**alad **s**andwiches **a**nd **r**emain **y**oung.
- **rhythm** = **r**hythm **h**as **y**our **t**wo **h**ips **m**oving.

Challenge

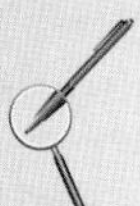

C8

Look at the tricky words below and see if you can devise your own mnemonics to help you remember them. It helps if your mnemonic starts with the word itself (like the rhythm example) or is linked to the word in meaning, e.g. the 'p' of parliament might be about politicians. (You might just devise a trick for the most difficult part of the word.)

- jealous
- science
- eight
- miniature
- field
- believe
- beautiful
- mountain
- parliament
- embarrass

Memory tricks 2

Sometimes we can remember how to spell words by learning the sequence of letters from other words, e.g. **-ight** and making a list of all the words that end like this, e.g. night, light, bright. Sometimes a mnemonic helps too, e.g. I go home tonight.

Challenge

C8

Make a list of words that end with **-ould** and **-ough**.

Memory tricks 3

With some words, saying them as they look on the page helps us to remember them:

e.g. Wednesday = Wed nes day.

This is when we exaggerate the part of the word (syllable) that we don't usually hear in speech.

Challenge

C8

How many other tricky words can you think of that 'spell speak' would help with?

Memory tricks 4

Some spellers use picture clues to help them remember spellings:

e.g. test tube

Challenge

C8

Can you devise some picture clues for the following words?

- square
- temperature
- pentagon
- geography
- triangle
- technology
- thermometer

Challenge 9: *spell magic!*

Below is an example of a puzzle that tests your spelling and understanding of the meanings of different words, e.g.:

Puzzle = something you might write on (5 letters) ....
Answer = board.

Challenge

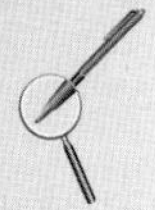

C9

Can you work out the following word puzzles?

A word meaning men, women and children. .... (6 letters)
Not a copy, this is the .... (8 letters)
Something you might write about your life in. .... (5 letters)
A season that comes just before winter. .... (6 letters)
A word to suggest a rough first drawing. .... (6 letters)
A very hot place. .... (6 letters)
A pudding. .... (7 letters)
A group of singers in church. .... (5 letters)

Challenge

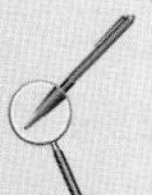

C9

Now you've had some practice, make your own list of words and devise some word puzzles for your partner.